Love you
Rush -
Lathan Hudson
Hi mi Nami AOL.

256 391 6231

once upon a time ...

There Was A Tavern

Volume 1

once upon a time ...

There Was A Tavern

Volume 1

By Lathan Hudson

Published by Lulu, Inc.

ISBN 978-1-304-12233-9

Published by Lulu, Inc.
Printed in the United States of America

Dedication

Jim & Jon Hager

This book is dedicated to two of the funniest guys I've ever met. The late Jon & Jim Hager befriended me and gave me the nickname "COACH." They never once wavered in their attempts to do the large and small things which bond friends.

We fished together...we recorded songs together...we hung out together and shared a comradeship which few can claim. Although Jon & Jim left this world way, way too early in life, the mark they put on their time spent here is indelible, and I would like to say that I loved them both as if they were my brothers.

This book is also dedicated to my special music friends who have passed on. I hope to join them in that Big Musical Gathering in the Great Beyond. The music there will take on a new definition: Ethereal Country Music.

Acknowledgments

Red Lane, Don Gant, & Pete Drake are three of the biggest reasons for any success I ever had in the music industry, and I owe them more than words can say.

Thanks to my family for their love, patience, and encouragement during the time I was occupied with this endeavor.

Thanks also to Janet Moreland, my close friend of twelve years, who has supported all of my writings as my literary agent, editor, technical assistant, and formatting expert, as well as being a shoulder to lean on whenever I felt blocked out (writers and authors will know and understand what this means.)

Earl Culver, I thank you for the awesome artwork you did for the covers of ... *There Was a Tavern*.

Contents

Stories

Prologue

Imagine that you could be magically transported back to the early-to-mid-1960s and you're sitting at the bar of this quaint, obscure tavern called "Kountry Korner." It was just one of many gathering-places, but a very special "watering hole" in the early sixties to the mid-seventies for some of the great songwriters and recording artists who would meet and *hold court* to play their music for one another. It was then located on 16th Avenue on Music Row in Nashville, Tennessee.

Music Row was then a small community and most of the recording, publishing, production, and record-pressing business was done in a four or five block area with each block being about three-fourths of a mile long. Old houses were converted into multi-million dollar businesses, and sometimes the outside of the house was left unfettered while the inside was decorated with all the comforts of home. Almost every songwriter-of-note knew each other and the only real rivalry was to get songs recorded by major recording artists.

It wasn't uncommon for writers to meet at the end of the day at a local watering hole and brag about their new song that had just been written or was on "hold" or had just been "cut" by a major artist. Much valuable information was often passed along at these "meetings."

Quietly, in walks **Kris Kristofferson** carrying his guitar case. Soon-to-be music legends **Harlan Howard, Hank Cochran, Red Lane, Shel Silverstein,** and others are already at a table drinking beer, spirits, or their beverages of choice. **Bobby Bare, Mel Tillis, Faron Young, Waylon Jennings,** and a few other established recording artists are there for the camaraderie, the music, the beer and spirits. Guitar cases are leaning up against the wall waiting for their contents to be uncrated, and you just know something exciting is about to happen.

You already have the advantage of knowing who the songwriters are; you also know that some of their best songs haven't even been written or recorded yet. You can't say a word to any of them. All you can do is listen …

Hardly any mention is made of the fact that Kristofferson is one of the most educated men to ever walk the streets of Music Row. Everybody knows that Kris is brilliant, but so are Shel Silverstein, Harlan Howard, and Red Lane. The fact is they are brilliant to one another, and soon all of Nashville and the rest of the world will be finding out what some already know—their real genius lies in their gift of pouring their hearts out and baring their souls while touching yours with their songs.

Kris puts his guitar case in the corner with the others, pulls up a chair, and joins his companions at their table. They make small talk, but not all that much, because the songs they'll soon be singing will convey more in the three minutes of music than they can say to one another in a week of conversation.

Kris Kristofferson

Someone finally breaks the silence by un-crating their guitar and fine-tuning it. The rules are the same as always—you have to play the latest song you've written and you can't play one that's been recorded.

As Harlan, Hank, Shel, Red, Kris, and some new blood take their turn reaching inside your soul, twisting your psyche, rerouting all the channels of every mind process you ever thought you had under control until you've become a part of each of their songs, you finally realize you have been holding your breath for a long, long time and only when the waitress asks if you'll have another beer do you come to your senses.

Welcome to the world of the Nashville songwriter and country music the way it was back when ...

Foreword 1

...Why me, Lord—what have I ever done—to deserve even one—of the pleasures I've known...? (By Kris Kristofferson, Publisher: Combine Music, Nashville, Tennessee)

One purpose for my writing this book is to acknowledge the sometimes-comical, sometimes-absurd, but almost-always earnest exploits of the Legends and Near-Legends of Country Music: songwriters, recording artists, and possibly just ordinary music people (that's gotta be the opposite of an oxymoron) that I was either befriended by, came in contact with, or heard stories about in my years of living in Nashville, Tennessee.

There are distinct, memorable things that separated these heroes of mine from the rest of the pack. Some of these are funny, some are sad, and some are just plain weird. Included are short stories, quotes and near-quotes and a few pictures from some of the greatest people (in my opinion) that ever loved country music, tuned a guitar, strummed a "C" Chord, and/or wrote a sad song that left an indelible scar on my soul.

Katie Hudson, Sharon Osuna, Lathan Hudson, Theresa Hudson

To me, it's a shame that, in the town that garners most of the credit for introducing Country Music to the world, there don't seem to be many real characters left. If there are any, maybe because of the medium of television and the advent of music videos, the so-called characters seem contrived and artificial. It could be that I'm just too old and tired to look for them, but it also seems that the New Guard or the younger Artists are too busy mining the gold that early writers, singers, and musicians left there than to take the time to really feel what they are writing or singing about, to take real chances, and "let it all hang out."

The personal secretary to Jerry Kennedy, record producer and then-head of Mercury Records, Nashville division, gave me some advice that helped get me through my stay in Nashville. What she imparted to me should be on some kind of a plaque in the courtyard of the Country Music Hall Of Fame building and should read thusly:

> *You will never show this town anything it hasn't already seen. Just find a musical stream; get in it, and everything you need to know about this wonderful adventure we call music will flow around you many times. When it does, gather what you missed the first few times until you find a comfort zone in which you can exist. That will be your career. Never waste your energy being disappointed, because what is meant to be will never pass you by.*

I soon learned and was taught by some of the best music people in the world to approach my craft of music like it was a mysterious journey and not a destination.

Please correct me if I'm right (copyrighted saying owned by Lathan Hudson), but I doubt that today's music people will ever leave a mark so indelible that their peers will be passing down their stories and exploits for generations to come.

If you get the impression that I don't like today's Country Music, nothing could be further from the truth. The truth is I *just don't recognize* today's Country Music.

It's sad to me that there aren't any more Kountry Korner Taverns in Nashville; at least, the way we knew them to be. Nashville does have music listening rooms where musical talent can be showcased, but in these rooms the talent is auditioned for and scrutinized, almost to the point of sterility. I think the principal criteria for listening room talent is that the participants have to be very young and very good-looking. *To qualify—send a glossy eight-by-ten, and we'll email you if you're good-looking enough to be accepted ...*

I'm sure my Nashville predecessors said some of the same things I'm saying, but today's Music community seems to have lost its warmth. The projected personality is like stale cornbread; it's way too slick and too business-like for my taste. Maybe that's the price of progress.

I liken it to a line from one of Joni Mitchell's songs, ... *they paved paradise and put up a parking lot...* or John Prine singing, ... *I'm sorry my son, but you're too late for asking—Mr. Peabody's coal train has hauled it away.* My own analogy is, ... *while we weren't looking, somebody slipped in and Bronzed Country Music's Gold medal ...*

I'm a child of the 50s and the 60s. I realize that change in almost everything is inevitable. That doesn't mean that change is always good. If some of my words seem harsh in this section, it's only because nostalgia plays a big part in my life and, with the exception of opinions I have solicited, what I have written here is strictly my perception.

From 1976 to 1994 I lived in Nashville, Tennessee and heard, first-hand, great stories about—and sometimes was privileged to be around—some of the real characters of Country Music. I can honestly say that at least one of my lifelong dreams was fulfilled, and to have witnessed what I feel is the last bastion of a dying breed of special people, I consider myself *A Lucky Man.*

I'll attempt to introduce you to some of these "heroes" of mine and tell some of their stories I heard—as well as some I was a part of—while living in the **Country Music Capitol of the World.**

Bobby Bare   **Dolly Parton**   **Larry Kingston**

I know I will have left a bunch of great stories and great people out, and just when this manuscript goes to press, I'll snap my fingers and say to myself, *Dummy! Why didn't you mention this person— or tell that story?*

For those of you who are not in this book, please know that the omission is purely accidental. Believe me when I say that you are in my heart and that you may be one of the main reasons my life has been blessed.

To quote Kris Kristofferson, *We may never pass this way again.* And to paraphrase John Hartford, ... *What's the difference being different when it's different now that looks alike...* Red Lane may have said it best with these immortal words, ... *Hoss, sometimes you just gotta wash your ass!*

Foreword 2

(every songwriter should know …)
How to Write a #1 Hit Song

I guess I've been in the music business professionally since 1973 beginning as a (very mediocre) singer in Birmingham, Alabama bars to writing songs in Nashville, Tennessee, producing records and conducting seminars on music and the business of music all over the USA.

I wasn't a bad songwriter, record producer, or speaker on the seminar or forum circuit which took me to places like Boise, Idaho ... Birmingham, Alabama ... Montgomery, Alabama ... Mobile, Alabama ... Houston, Texas ... Slidell, Louisiana … Pine Bluff, Arkansas … Macon, Georgia … and many other venues.

Lathan Hudson in concert

We lived in Nashville for eighteen years, and I spent the biggest part of that time concentrating primarily on my songwriting. After we left Nashville (and even while we were there), I would either read or hear about some of my music buddies or former buddies and their successes. Sometimes they would either be a guest on a television show or a radio program and the host or moderator would invariably ask them how many *Number One Songs* they had written.

Sometimes I would hear them say something like this ... *Well, Ralph, I've written 26 Number One Songs.*

I would say to myself, *Oh my God*! I knew this individual, and when I left Nashville in 1994, he hadn't written his First Number One Song, much less 26! He must have really *turned-it-on* with the creative juices after I left town! *I've got to know his secret!*

I'd like to say, first, that I've written or co-written, two World-wide Number One Songs, but after listening to some of my buddies' interviews, I've reassessed my thinking concerning what constitutes a Number One Song.

Further into these television and radio interviews with my buddies, I found out things like: *Yes, Ralph, my next door neighbor's son recorded a song in his bedroom studio that I wrote, and he took it to our local radio station and, believe-it-or-not, they played that 'sucker' until it was declared the Number One Song on Station* WSUX *for-a-day in my hometown of Backwash, Oregon.*

Another time, I was driving through the Rockies when I heard another one of my buddies being interviewed.

Same question. How many Number One Songs have you written? *Well, Charlie-Mac, I heard one of my songs being played off of Billy Blueblood's album—now, mind you, it wasn't even his 'single' at the time—and the Dee Jay said, 'Our station manager was listening to some of old Billy Blueblood's songs and said that my song, Dance with the Dude who Drove You to the Prom, was really the best song on this here album, and they declared that it was going to be their Number One Song-for-a-day, because it had beaten the former 'Number One Song for-a-day' (My Gal Don't Give Out Her Number to Nobody No More) by two airplays last Thursday'— and, Charlie-Mac, all told, I guess I've written 26 ... or maybe even 27 Number One Songs.*

Like I said, I started reassessing my thinking concerning what constitutes a Number One Song and I've had ... wait! let me think a minute ... I guess I've written, or co-written, EXACTLY ... **two.**

My views on becoming/being a songwriter are well known among my music buddies. The following is part of a memo from the desk of Brad Reaves, president of the Birmingham, Alabama Songwriters' Association:

A thanks also goes to publisher/writer Lathan Hudson and I'll close with these thoughts from his spring visit....

THE TWELVE STAGES OF BEING A SONGWRITER

1. I'm not in it for the money, I just want to hear my song on the radio.

2. My songs are better than what I hear on the radio!

3. I finally got my song published. I need it recorded.

4. I just got my first song recorded. I hope it makes the album.

5. My song made the album. I hope it's a single.

6. It's a single. I hope it makes the billboard charts.

7. a. IT MADE THE CHARTS. I HOPE IT GOES TOP TEN.
   b. IT MADE TOP TEN! I HOPE IT GOES NUMBER 1.

8. IT'S A NUMBER 1 RECORD. I HOPE IT WINS AN AWARD!

9. It didn't win an award. It came in fifth.

10. My song was better than the other four.

11. I hear my song on the radio all the time. SO WHAT!

12. I don't write these songs for free. WHERE'S MY MONEY????

A special thanks to you members that are always there for critique sessions and ideas.

                                        President
                                        Brad Reaves

P.S.

OUR CHRISTMAS PARTY WILL BE OUR DECEMBER 4TH MEETING. IT WILL BE HELD AT 7:15 AT THE TERRACE RESTAURANT IN FIVE POINTS. (1813 10TH ST. SOUTH...BY THE SOUTHSIDE BAPTIST CHURCH ON THE ONE-WAY STREET, 939-0201). THEIR MENU INCLUDES WINE AND BEER (BYOB FOR LIQUOR), DINNERS $9-$11, SANDWICHES $5, AND APPETIZERS. LADIES NIGHT OUT (BIRMINGHAM'S SIX PIECE FEMALE A CAPPELLA GROUP), WILL DO A 40 MINUTE SET). FRIENDS AND VISITORS ARE WELCOME.

Once Upon a Time ...

There Was a Tavern

Volume 1

Stories

Chapter 1

Country Music Does Not Cure Cancer

L-R Dan Wilson, Sparky Lawrence, Don Gant, Lathan Hudson (1977)

Don Gant came into my life in 1977. I had been in Nashville for one year, and Don was then vice-president of Tree Publishing Company. At the time, Tree was the largest country music publishing company in the world.

The Tree building was a magical, mysterious place to me because I had been trying with some limited success to get my songs listened to at smaller publishing companies. I had even had a few of my songs recorded by some minor artists, but I didn't think I was quite ready for Tree, which was the publishing ocean where the big fish swam, because I had barely gotten my feet wet in the smaller ponds.

One day I was in the lobby of the Tree building with a buddy of mine from Dothan, Alabama, who was a friend of Sonny Throckmorton. Sonny was a staff writer for Tree, and at the time was one of the hottest writers in town, meaning that his songs were in demand, and he was getting them recorded almost as fast as he could write them.

Anyway, Sonny came down to the lobby and my friend

introduced me to him. After they had swapped a few stories, my friend told Sonny that I was a good songwriter and, believe it or not, Sonny grabbed a guitar that was leaning against the wall of the room we were in and asked me to play something.

I had just written a novelty song called *Leaving Love All Over The Place* and played it for Sonny. Sonny grabbed me by the arm and took me upstairs. He introduced me to Don Gant and said, "Don, you need to listen to some of this boy's songs. He's a good writer."

Some of Tree's staff writers and some of their hit songs at the time—just to name a few—were **Curly Putman**: *Green, Green Grass Of Home ... My Elusive Dreams ... He Stopped Loving Her Today ... Golden Ring*—**Bobby Braddock**: *He Stopped Loving Her Today ... Golden Ring ... Her Name Is* —**Red Lane**: *Blackjack County Chain ... Till I Get It Right ... Miss Emily's Picture*—**Sterling Whipple**: *Blind Man In The Bleachers ... Forever Lovers*—**Harlan Howard**: *I've Got A Tiger By The Tail ... Busted ... I Fall To Pieces ... Heartaches By The Number*—**Hank Cochran**: I *Fall To Pieces ... A Little Bitty Tear Let Me Down ... Ocean Front Property*—**Sonny Throckmorton**: *I Wish I Was Eighteen Again ... Trying To Love Two Women ... Knee Deep In Loving You*. Also, some of Tree's former songwriters were **Willie Nelson** and **Roger Miller**. You get the picture. The reason song titles appear by more than one name is that co-writing is a common practice among songwriters.

I was standing there, feeling naked surrounded by the living ghosts of all those songwriting legends and soon-to-be-legends. Almost all are now *Hall of Famers*, and, on the strength of hearing one song, Sonny Throckmorton was telling Don Gant that I was a good songwriter.

Don was cordial enough, and we set up an appointment for me to play some songs for him for publishing consideration. One of the first songs I played for Don was *Leaving Love All Over The Place*. We signed the standard publishing agreement, which gave Tree Publishing permission to pitch designated songs of mine to record producers and artists for recording consideration. In return, if a song was recorded, a more formal contract would be signed to replace the initial agreement.

A few days later Don called me at home and told me that George Jones had recorded my song, *Leaving Love All Over The Place*.

I'm almost sure that I thanked him and then just stood there, holding the phone for what seemed like a week.

A few months after George Jones' album was released, someone brought to my attention the latest issue of ROLLING STONE Magazine. There was a review of George Jones' *Bartender Blues* album. One of the songs featured was my song, *Leaving Love All Over The Place*. The ROLLING STONE editor wrote that *Leaving Love...* was the "**most explicit S&M** (sado-masochistic) **Country song that he had heard in quite some time**." For a long time I thought *S & M* meant Spanish & Mexican. I caught a lot of good-natured ribbing from my buddies.

Excerpt from 1979 Rolling Stone Magazine Country Music Review:

Bartender's Blues, for example, contains the world's first George Jones disco tune. As if that weren't enough, the album includes the most explicit S&M song I've heard in quite some time. In the hands of any other performer, numbers like these would merely be silly, but with Jones and his emotion-charged voice, you're never able to tell whether he's joking or whether he might really mean it.

Who else could?—or would?—sing lines like these from "Leaving Love All over the Place":

"The lady at the roomin' house served our eviction notice yesterday ... /She said it'd take a dozen carpenters to fix the broken bed and hang the drapes/ But we just never learned to love without leavin' love all over the place."

Sounds stupid, right? Well, I won't reveal the song's surprise ending, but the way Jones sings it, it's halfway scary.

I soon signed a staff songwriter contract with Tree, making them my exclusive publisher, and even that was an adventure in the sardonic wit of Don Gant. After some initial success as a free-lance writer with Tree being a good customer for me, I approached Don and told him I wanted to be a staff writer for Tree. When Don asked me *why?*, I told him that I wanted my song catalog to be in one place and in the event of my passing, my family wouldn't have to trace my publishing trail all over Nashville looking for my songs.

Don just looked at me and said, "Why should you care? You'll be dead."

Even his saying that carried some truth, which I perceived to be his wit and sometimes infinite, however misguided, wisdom.

As a staff writer for Tree, I attempted to apply what Jerry Kennedy's secretary had told me and tried to fit in—kind of like a football player with a good attitude sitting on the bench trying to catch the coach's eye and hoping he'd put you in the game.

Tree was inundated with characters. **Don Cook** (who, at this writing, is the very successful record producer for the multi-award winning country duo of Brooks and Dunn) used to play bass guitar in musical shows at Opryland. Sometimes when crowds were sparse, he'd play while lying on his back.

Rafe Van Hoy (nickname "Ralph," then child guitar pickin'/songwriting prodigy)

Sonny Throckmorton (Sonny calls everybody "Puddin" and everybody calls Sonny "Puddin." Sonny has this funny, high-pitched laugh that all of his friends try to imitate)

Bobby Braddock (near-genius). (**Bobby** and **Rafe** were not allowed on the third floor of the Tree building because once they urinated in Tree owner **Buddy Killen's** goldfish pond. **Buddy** had a *huge* goldfish pond on the third floor filled with expensive and exotic fish. They killed all the goldfish.)

Bobby Braddock Brings "Bums" To Buddy's Bash ...

Also, there was the time that **Buddy Killen** was hosting a VIP party for executives from the major record labels in Nashville, and **Bobby Braddock** took his van to the Mission Home down on *lower Broadway* and loaded it with *derelicts* and *down-and-outers—the less-*

fortunate people who were there looking for a warm meal and a place to sleep at night—and brought them into the Tree building; took them upstairs to the party; fed them, and introduced each one to Buddy Killen and the many guests who were wearing name-tags.

Braddock said, "Me and my entourage were on first-name basis with nearly everyone before the party ended abruptly."

Bruce Channel (Bruce wrote and sang the mega-hit song *Hey, Hey Baby,* which gained a new breath of life by appearing in the movie "Dirty Dancing," whose soundtrack sold more than twenty-five million copies. Everybody calls **Bruce** "Bro," and he's one of the most likeable human beings alive. Don Gant called **Bruce** one of the greatest *live* entertainers ever.)

Sterling Whipple (unpretentiously funny guy who was forever trying to figure out the "meaning" of life). Sterling had an unparalleled work ethic, and everyone commented on it. If a new pharmaceutical product appeared on the market, Don Gant would say, "Let Sterling try it first."

Rock Killough (Rock was a Charlie Weaver look-alike who could play any instrument that made music and was a terrific singer/songwriter.)

Alan Rhody (Rhody was a quiet, unassuming tall red-haired kid of German descent who had spent time as a guest of Canada, because of his strong beliefs about not wanting to get involved in a jungle skirmish in an unpopular police action in a small country somewhere in Southeast Asia. Rhody's ambition was to be a recording artist first and songwriter second, but, unfortunately, fate had other plans. At the time he was enjoying a #1 hit single by the Oak Ridge Boys called *I'll Be True To You,* he would have to put his artist plans on hold.) (The Oak Ridge Boys were a popular Gospel-turned-Country group of the 70s & 80s with hit songs: *Elvira ... I'll Be True To You ... Y'all Come Back Saloon ... Trying To Love Two Women ...* and *Thank God For Kids.)*

Red Lane (Red was so laid-back that jokes circulated about him because of his mysterious presence, or lack-thereof.)

Red Lane is sucking his teeth...

Once I walked into Don Gant's office and the usual gang was there. Don Gant put his finger up to his lips for me to be quiet when I came in. They were gathered 'round the telephone and had it on speaker. I asked them what they were doing, and Don whispered that they were listening to Red Lane "suck his teeth." Red had a habit of calling you, and after he said, "Hello," he would wait for you to do all the talking, and he would hold the phone forever, and eventually you would be duped into a one-sided conversation with Red doing all the listening. He had called Don from Texas, and every few minutes Red would suck his teeth, sounding like *sss-ff-t*. Each time he would do it, the whole gang would snicker under their breath. Some things are funny, and I guess for some others to be funny, you *had to be there*.

The mystique of Don Gant...

Don Gant and I became what I consider to be *great* friends and played a lot of golf together. I played the last round of golf Don ever played. It was a week before his passing at age 44, and I can tell you for certain that any amount of time spent with Don was an adventure. He was a natural leader, even though he didn't relish the role. Almost anyone who ever had any dealings with Don just naturally migrated to him, and his approval or disapproval could *make* or *break* almost any of his followers' days. I reckoned it was because he could comfortably play the dual role of executive and *good-old-boy*. At Tree he was the liaison between songwriter and upper-office management; primarily Buddy Killen, owner of Tree Publishing.

About a week before Don's passing, we agreed to meet at Hermitage Golf course. I'd sometimes ask him if we needed anyone to join us, and he'd say, *Nah! Just me and you, son*.

Don Gant and I were the same age, but he always called me *son,* and I dubbed him *Mr. Grant*. As close as I felt to Don, who I considered one of my best friends, nobody ever really got too close.

We walked the golf course and caddied our clubs with a pull cart. Hardly anyone was on the course that day, so we played *hole number one* twice because we didn't like the way our games had started. On hole number *nine,* we met up with Noel Fox. Noel was the manager of The Oak Ridge Boys' music publishing company and had actually sang bass as a former Oak Ridge Boy. Noel joined us for the rest of the round.

Segue—managing a music publishing company is easy...

I had in recent weeks taken a song to Noel Fox at the Oak Ridge Boys publishing company that one of my favorite co-writers, Angela Kaset, and I had written called *The Dollmaker.* (Angela Kaset is a multi-talented singer/songwriter whose biggest hit song at this printing is *I'm Looking For Something In Red* by Lorrie Morgan. Angela also had a hit song of the same title as an artist on Chrysalis Records.) The song tells of a Rag Doll sitting on a shelf beside a beautiful China Doll, and the Rag Doll wishes she would love him like he loves her. Thanks to the Dollmaker (in the song), she does fall in love with the Rag Doll.

Noel loved the song, and I left a copy for him to play for any artist that he might think the song might serve to be a hit. Jim Ed Brown had used the song as an opening and closing theme for a television show hosted by him and his wife Becky. (The show was about Jim Ed and Becky Brown visiting RV Parks all over the U.S. and was called "Going Our Way.")

A few days later I checked my telephone answering machine. Apparently some or all of the members of the Oak Ridge Boys had stopped by their publishing company and Noel had been in the process of playing songs for them to consider recording on their upcoming album. Noel had mentioned to me that *The Dollmaker* might be a sweet song for The Oaks (as they were called) because, even though it wasn't lyrically similar to the song they had scored a big hit written by Eddy Raven called *Thank God For Kids,* the "flavor" of the song was in the same musical vein. I need also to explain that The Oaks liked to *re-e-lax* and—hoping not to sound libelous—sometimes, not necessarily because William Lee Golden (one of the members) actually lived in a teepee, smoke clouds would fill the rooms they were in.

About the third message into my answering machine was Noel Fox's unmistakable booming bass voice saying,...*Uh! Lathan ... This is, uh ... Noel. I can't find my copy of the song called ... Uh! ... I can't think of the title of it ... Uh! ... I'll call you back when I can ... Uh! ... think of it ...*

So much for another fleeting brush with fame and fortune. I can still smell the smoke.

Fore ...

Don Gant was a riot on the golf course. There wouldn't be anyone within five hundred yards of us and he'd walk right up to me, make a ball of both of his fists, stretch his arms down by his side, and loudly whisper in my ear, "I hate Germans. Don't you hate them f...ing Europeans?"

By then, Don had started his own publishing company which was being funded by Germans and Europeans. Don *was* not one to ever hide his feelings about anything. You always knew where he stood on any issue, and that was one of the things that made him unique.

On *hole number ten*, Don hit his second shot in the water. He took every club out of his bag and started throwing them in all directions, all the time screaming expletives. Noel Fox and I were lying on the ground "laughing our asses off."

Don would yell at the top of his lungs, "I hate this f ... ing game! I'm a mental midget! F ... k Germans and Europeans!"

Then with his last club in hand, he beat it on the ground and ranted and raved some more.

Noel and I picked up Don's clubs and put them back in the bag while he was yelling, "I hate this f ... ing game!"

After Don had cooled off somewhat, the round continued. On *hole number eleven*, Don chipped his golf ball in the hole for a "birdie," and he paraded around the green and proclaimed, "Isn't this a beautiful day? Isn't this a great game?"

They say a round of golf will reveal a man's true character. They also say that life sometimes gives people warnings, and I really believe that on the day of our last round of golf Don had been given one of those warnings. Don had played basketball in high school and had broken his foot in one of the games. He talked about his broken foot all through the round of golf that day. I asked him if it was bothering him, and he said *No!* but continued to talk about how he had broken his foot.

Don and Ron Chancey, who was one of Don's best friends and the record producer for the Oak Ridge Boys, had planned to go to Destin, Florida to play some golf the following week. We had talked about the weather report and how it was raining all through that part of Florida. One minute Don would say he was going and another minute he would say he wasn't going because they wouldn't be able to play golf. Ron Chancey had a boat in a marina at Destin, Florida. Ron and a group of his friends would go and stay on his boat during the trip to their golf outings. Despite the foul weather warnings for most of the state of Florida, Don, his brother Ronnie, and Ron Chancey took the trip to Destin.

I was in the studio that week doing some demos of songs I had written and got a phone call. It was Noel Fox. Noel asked me if I had heard about Don Gant. He said that Don had stepped onto Ron Chancey's boat and broke his foot (the same foot we had talked about at our golf game). I kinda laughed it off until Noel said that they weren't expecting Don to live through the night. I couldn't figure it out. Noel then told me that the re-break of his foot had sent a massive supply of tiny blood clots all through Don's lungs, and he was at the hospital with little or no chance for survival.
My world stopped!

The next morning I grabbed a newspaper and read through it and for some reason figured if Don wasn't in the paper, things would be okay. My father-in-law came by and asked me if I had read about Don Gant? I told him I read the paper but saw nothing. I had missed a page.
On one of the back pages was an article that read "**Don Gant, Record Producer, dies at age 44**." I took a shower and for the first time since I was a kid, cried my eyes completely dry.

Don Gant was the most intriguing man I believe I ever met. He was my friend. He was my mentor He was a hero to a lot of songwriters. I'm not ashamed to say I loved him.

I saved the golf scorecard of the last round Don and I played together and a golf ball that Don fished out of the water and gave to me. I have them mounted on my wall like a trophy. Of all the awards I have been afforded in music and sports, this is one of my two most treasured.

Hole	Hcp	1	2	3	4	5	6	7	8	9	Out	10	11	12	13	14	15	16	17	18	In	Tot	Net
Gold		350	550	206	390	216	380	410	500	443	3445	385	600	331	185	410	360	550	165	344	3330	6775	
Blue		336	530	191	380	190	360	390	485	423	3285	369	580	321	170	392	347	531	153	335	3198	6483	
White		310	505	180	370	157	340	360	480	386	3068	349	480	305	152	375	325	520	132	305	2943	6011	
Handicap		18	8	16	6	12	14	10	4	2		9	1	11	13	5	17	3	15	7			
LATHAN											41										41	82	
DON GANT											45										40	85	
Par		4	5	3	4	3	4	4	5	4	36	4	5	4	3	4	4	5	3	4	36	72	
Red		275	470	130	350	147	316	325	420	360	2793	317	443	295	135	355	290	481	97	269	2682	5475	
Handicap		18	8	16	6	12	14	10	4	2		9	1	11	13	5	17	3	15	7			

Scorecard of last round of golf Lathan Hudson & Don Gant ever played together, 1987

Don Gant had cut his musical teeth at ACUFF-ROSE Publishing. Fred Rose and Roy Acuff started ACUFF-ROSE Publishing. Fred Rose and Gene Autry were friends and business partners and ACUFF-ROSE Publishing was, at the time, the second largest country music publishing company in the world.

Don was a maverick's maverick. He was his own man and just did not conform to many things. He once told us the story about why he left ACUFF-ROSE music. At ACUFF-ROSE Publishing, Don was a record producer and a songwriter. Don even had success as a recording artist and was one of the most sought-after background singers in town. He said one day he decided he would resign and Wesley Rose (Fred's brother) asked him why.

Don said, "Wesley, I can't come to work here every day wishing that you'd die so I could have your job."

Don's recording career was short and successful. He was part of a duo strangely enough called NEON PHILHARMONIC. Don's partner was Tupper Saucy. Tupper was a study in human behavior and

10

was at least as much the maverick as his singing partner. They had one hit song titled *Morning Girl.* Don was the lead singer and had a beautiful voice. The song is a hauntingly moving ballad asking the question about the life and a single night of a teenage girl. They also played some hotel venues in Las Vegas, but Don said he didn't care for the life of a recording artist. He liked to sleep in his own bed at night.

As a background singer, Don and his friend, Bergen White, who is also a famous Nashville music string-arranger, provided the background vocals on the mega-hit song *You Picked A Fine Time To Leave Me Lucille,* co-written by Hal Bynum and Roger Bowling and sung by Kenny Rogers.

One of Don's subsequent jobs was vice-president and head of A&R for ABC-DOT Records, Nashville division. He produced the first four albums on Jimmy Buffet. He told a great story about his so-called musical acumen. Don said they had gathered all of the songs for Buffet's album *Living And Dying In Three-Quarter Time.* On the eve of going in the studio to record, Jimmy brought Don a new song he had just written and wanted to include it on the album. Don reminded Buffet how they had meticulously picked the ten songs that they were going to record for the album, but that he would listen to his new song and decide if they needed to replace it (with the new song).

Jimmy Buffet played Don his new song called *Come Monday.* Don said that he looked Buffet in the eye and said, "Jimmy, that's a piece of crap."

The rest is music history. *Come Monday* became Buffet's first big hit and his *breakout song* and when Don would tell us the story, he'd self-deprecatingly say, "Shows you how f ... ing much I know about music."

Don also discovered a famous recording group. I never tired of listening to Don tell the story. He said while he was the head of ABC-DOT Records this group from Memphis, Tennessee brought him a recording of one of their songs. Don said he really liked the song and wanted to sign them to the label and put the record out on them. He made the call to California or New York (wherever the label was based) and told the *heads* at ABC-DOT that he had discovered this group and wanted to put a record out on them. Naturally, the *powers-that-be* wanted to hear the group and the song, so Don played their recording (that they had recorded in a garage in Memphis) over the phone. What followed was typical *musical tampering* dialogue.

> **Powers-That-Be**: *We're not spending money to sign this piece of crap to our label. The song is awful, the group is worse.*
> **Don Gant**: *Well, if I can't sign an act to the label, what am I doing here? F ... k you, I quit!"*
> Don slams down the phone.
> **Powers-That-Be** call **Don** back and say: *Okay, we'll sign the group to a one-song deal and if the song doesn't 'fly', you won't have to quit. You'll be fired.*
> **Don Gant**: *Okay*!

Well, the story goes that Don signed the group and put the song out, and the song immediately took off and became a monster hit.

The group was THE AMAZING RHYTHM ACES, and the song was *Third Rate Romance—Low Rent Rendezvous;* the producer of the group was the late guitar playing great Barry 'Byrd' Burton and lead singer was Russell Smith.

> **Don Gant** gets on the phone to the **Powers-That-Be** and says: *I've been thinking about the way you jerked me around. You can't talk to me that way. F ... k every one of you. I quit.*
> Again, Don slams down the phone.
> **Powers-That-Be** call Don back and say: *If you'll stay at ABC-DOT, we'll give you a $10,000 per year raise.*
> **Don Gant**: *Okay!*
> **Don Gant** calls **Powers-That-Be** back and says: *I've been thinking about this, and you assholes can't buy me. F ... k every one of you. I quit!*
> Don slams down the phone.

I think that's when Don left and was hired at Tree Publishing. When Don left Tree Publishing to pursue his own business of owning and running a publishing company (*funded by f...ing Germans*), as soon as my writing contract was up at Tree Publishing (for some reason the good times just didn't seem as good), I started looking for employment elsewhere.

Softball is an important game...

**Warner Brothers Softball Team; bottom row, third from left:
Lathan Hudson**

Softball was a big deal in music in my early years in Nashville, and many of the publishing companies and record labels had their own teams. They played each other in games and tournaments and would spend thousands of dollars on uniforms and the criteria was that to be eligible to play in tournaments, a player had to be employed in music in some capacity. Publishing companies and record companies would sometimes hire good softball players to work for them just to have them on their team. *Bragging rights* among the publishers and record labels was a big thing. A twenty-dollar trophy was worth hundreds of times more to the publisher or record label if it was sitting on their mantel or hanging on their office wall.

I was a pretty good softball and baseball player when I signed a staff writing agreement with Pete Drake Publishing Company. Coincidentally, Pete had two softball teams, and I was made player-manager for one and played for the other. Sometimes we'd play four to five ballgames per week during the spring, summer, and fall. I later found out that a friend of mine, Tony Naile, had told Pete that I was a good ball player, and he should hire me as a songwriter so I could play for his team, and that was the biggest reason for my being there.

In Search of an Epiphany...

Like I said, I would visit Don just to listen to his stories and the latest words of wisdom he would pass down. Occasionally, we would go golfing or just take a ride in his car and talk.

Creative people are constantly searching for an "epiphany," or as Webster puts it, ... a breakthrough of transcendent awareness .... I think Don Gant and I experienced one together while just riding the streets of Music Row in his Oldsmobile and talking. A Dolly Parton song was playing on the car radio, and for some reason it broke into our conversation as if someone had broad-sided his vehicle with a bulldozer. The lines from Dolly's song hit Don and me at the same moment, and he just pulled his car off the road, and we just looked at one another for what seemed an eternity. Dolly was singing the lyrics to her then new song *If You Don't Think God Will Get You, Then You're Wrong.*
Don said to me, "Son, did you hear what I just heard?"
I said something back to him like, "I think so."

There was no real rhyme or reason for why it affected us at the same time like it did, but it was a suspended moment in time that I wish I could recapture because for the first time in a long time I felt the real impact of what a song could—or should—mean to a listener.

During one of our rides or talks I asked him why he had never approached me about writing for his publishing company. He had brought some writers from Tree Publishing whose contracts had run out and hired them to write for his company.

14

Don looked me in the eye and said, "Son ... ," (then he named some names that I won't mention but had been great writers with some big hit songs recorded by major artists at Tree) ... "they need me. You're pretty much your own person, and you don't need me like they do."

I have never been paid a greater compliment in my life. On the other end of the spectrum, I had never been so disappointed. I would have walked bare-footed through burning coals to have written songs for Don Gant's publishing company.

Reality Check ...

I had just had a song recorded by BJ Thomas, which I co-wrote with BJ's wife, Gloria, and my friend Red Lane. The song was titled *New Looks From An Old Lover*. It was getting a lot of radio and television airplay and would eventually go on to be a worldwide Number One Hit.

On one of my visits to Don's publishing company, I had just written a new song titled *In One Easy Moment* that I was proud of, and when I walked into Don's office, I announced to everyone there that I had just written my best song ever.

Don, in his best sardonic voice said to me, "Son, I just heard the best song you've ever written—on the radio today."

Touché!

There was a musical "trick" that I've had pulled on me so many times that I'm almost ashamed to admit it. First, you would bring a song into a crowded office to play for whoever was in the office at the time and would agree to listen. Invariably, someone would ask you to put the tape on the recorder (back then songs were recorded on reel-to-reel tape). While you were threading up the tape of your song—and while your back was turned—everyone would sneak out of the office and hide in the outer room. When you turned around, the room would be empty, and you would be sitting there with "egg" on your face.

One of Don Gant's favorite sayings was, "You didn't discover a cure for cancer; you only wrote a song."

To me, this covered the gamut of the arrogance of being a "special" songwriter from "A" to "Z."
Viola!

Unfortunately, some songwriters are arrogant and are made to feel privileged in many places because they have what some consider a unique talent. Fortunately, the majority of the really good songwriters are, for the most part, humble and stay much too busy writing and honing their craft to take the time to display too much arrogance.

Letter to Don Gant

Attn: Mr. Grant
Dear Don,

I have always taken your words of wisdom to heart, and I know I didn't discover a cure for Cancer, but I would like for you to read a Thank you for your letter to me from one of my friend's mother who recently had open-heart surgery.
I know you're probably up there somewhere making everyone laugh or driving them crazy. You were and still are my best friend.

I miss you.

Lathan

June 26, 1993

Dear Lathan,

Annette knew how much I had wanted to hear some of your songs, so she made me a tape of some you gave her.
I just wanted you to know how very talented you were. Your tape got me through a very bad night after my heart surgery; in fact that tape helped me watch the sunrise over St. Louis.

Every time I heard the songs, I realized how really beautiful they were. When I was being wheeled down a hall to my room after a big test, I heard one of your songs coming from the radio in one of the rooms. It lifted my spirits.

Thanks for being a friend to Annette. I do hope we can come down there before you move.

Thanks again,

Mary Kathryn Wiggins

"Thank You" letter to Lathan Hudson from
Mary Kathryn Wiggins

Lathan Hudson

p.s.—Mentality of a Songwriter ...

During the time I was walking the streets of Music Row trying to get my songs heard and with what little success came my way, in the interim, I was working as a heavy equipment operator with a company in Nashville called Hardaway Construction.

Just after I had gotten my George Jones song *Leaving Love All Over The Place* recorded (and hadn't heard a tape of the recording), I was operating a backhoe on a job where the company was constructing apartment complexes.

On this particular day I was digging "footers" (a long line of ditches where concrete is poured for the foundation to support the building), and this old guy nicknamed "Pappy" was walking along behind me shoveling the loose dirt from the ditch. Pappy had gotten mad at me the day before, and since he was an ex-convict, I just figured that was his nature and thought nothing of it, because the problem we had the day before seemed to have resolved itself.

I idled the engine down on the backhoe and swung the boom away from the ditch so I could step down from the machine. When I looked up, Pappy had a .38 Smith & Wesson short-nose pistol pointed about two feet from my head and right between my eyes.

Pappy said to me, "You think I've forgotten about yesterday, don't you?"

I didn't say anything.

He then said to me, "You don't think I'll kill you, do you?"

They say when a man is facing his mortality, sometimes his whole life flashes before him. I swear, all that was running through my mind was this: "I'm never going to get to hear George Jones sing my song." No fear ... no anything ... just, "I'm never going to get to hear George Jones sing my song."

About that time, the bosses on the job started running down the hill toward us shouting, "'Pappy, put that gun down right now!!"

Pappy turned to the bosses and said, "You don't think I'll kill him, do you?"

I started thinking, "Tell him 'yes' you think he'll kill me, so he'll put the gun down."

They finally talked Pappy out of his gun, and I immediately went to my car and went home. For some reason, they didn't report him to the police—all they did was send him to a job on the other side of Nashville.

About a week later, I was called to this job on the other side of Nashville, and the first person I saw while I was filling out some papers was Pappy. This guy was very old, and he walked up to me and asked how I was doing. I'm sure he didn't even recall the incident about the pistol.

I told the bosses I wasn't going to work that job, and they sent me to another job site where, when I looked the job over, there was no Pappy to be seen.

This is a true story and sometimes when I tell it to my friends, I think about the George Jones thought that ran through my head and wonder, "Are those thoughts the norm for a songwriter?" I wouldn't be surprised if they are.

Chapter 2

Dracula Only Comes Out At Night…

Pete Drake was affectionately known as Count Drakeula because of the nocturnal hours he kept when working at his recording studio. Pete was an *all-world* session pedal steel guitar player and famous record producer. His steel guitar can be heard on hundreds of records ranging from his own million-selling Instrumental hit song *Forever*, to songs by Elvis Presley, George Harrison, Bob Dylan, George Jones, Tammy Wynette, Johnny Paycheck, David Allen Coe, Johnny Duncan, Joe Stampley, Janie Fricke, and the list goes on. Oh, yes, and he was called to England on many occasions to record with a group called the Beatles.

Pete is credited for being single-handedly responsible for opening the entire pop and rock field to the sounds of the pedal steel. His single-string steel line accompaniment can be heard on many pop songs. Ringo Starr was a friend and a fan of Pete Drake. Pete produced Ringo's country album *Beaucoup Of Blues,* which was recorded at Pete's studio using Nashville Musicians. Initially, Ringo wanted Pete to come to England to produce the album, but Pete talked Ringo into recording in Nashville because of the talent pool of country musicians there.

Pete is also credited with inventing the "Talking" steel guitar, a method where a surgical hose was implemented from his steel guitar and attached to the corner of Pete's lips. Pete would mouth the lyrics to a song, and the sound would come through the steel guitar. It was, and still is, amazing.

Pete produced Grammy Award winning gospel albums on BJ Thomas'. He also produced two #1 Country Hits on BJ Thomas, *What Ever Happened To Old Fashioned Love* and *New Looks From An Old Lover*. Melba Montgomery was the recipient of Pete's production on her #1 award winning song *No Charge*, written by Harlan Howard.

Pete also produced award-winning albums on Boxcar Willie, George Hamilton IV, Bjoro Haaland, and many of the Grand Ole Opry greats.

When I signed a staff-writing contract with Pete Drake publishing companies, a brand new publishing company catalog was formed exclusively for my songs. The name of the company was **Petewood Music,** registered with ASCAP. The other staff writers were **Larry Kingston**, *Thank God And Greyhound You're Gone*; a #1 country hit by **Roy Clark** and **Harlan Sanders**, *If Drinking Don't Kill Me—Her Memory Will;* a #1 country hit by **George Jones**. As I mentioned, I managed and played for Pete's two softball teams. One of the teams was named **PETE'S FREAKS**—sounds 'bout right.

A Rose is a Rose is a Rose...

Pete's wife, Rose, was our publisher, and I'm at a safe enough distance from her to admit that Larry Kingston, Harlan Sanders, and I delighted in trying to drive her almost to the point of insanity. Rose was a beautiful, tall, red-haired woman and had been the victim of some playfully bad advice from some of the more successful publishers about town who would tell her how to treat her writers and then go off somewhere, drink beer and snicker, wondering if she took their direction. Sometimes she would attempt to put their *words of wisdom* into practice, and we would try and be ready to fend off the wolf-like advice she had been getting from the likes of Bill Hall (Hall-Clements Publishing), Bob Beckham (Combine Music), and Don Gant (Don Gant Music).

Once she called a staff meeting together for the sake of trying to cut down on our using too many office supplies such as pencils, pens, paper, and the like. Rose asked if any of us writers had any suggestions, and I raised my hand. After granting me the "floor," I proceeded to explain that if she would take blank paper and Xerox it, she would have twice as much blank paper, and it would save the company money.

Rose wrote down my suggestion, and the next day someone had apparently spilled-the-beans. Every time I would come near her she would give me an icy-stare.

21

Another time we were talking about individual oddities of some members of successful musical groups. It just so happened that Ray Sawyer of the Country-Rock group, Doctor Hook, had been at the Drake Music publishing company the day before. Ray is blind in one eye and wears a patch over his eye.

I asked Rose, "Do you know that sometimes, Ray, for a joke, will put the patch over his good eye and drive through the streets of Music Row with the top pulled back on his convertible just to fool his friends?"

She looked at me in amazement and said, "Really?"

The Nocturnal One ...

Pete Drake only came out at night. For the two years I wrote for his company, I don't remember seeing him but one or two times in the daytime, and I can't even swear to that. Pete was one of the nicest, unassuming people you would ever want to meet and/or do business with. He also had an arsenal of some great stories and quips. Pete kept everyone laughing. Aside from his obvious talent, it was easy to see why recording artists wanted him to produce them.

When Larry Kingston or Harlan Sanders and I would co-write a song, Pete would sometimes lend his expertise in helping us produce the demo. He would say things to me like, "Lathan, you always fail to amaze me."

Sometimes, before I would figure out what he said, I would thank him.

Often Pete would say to a guitar player who had messed up a lick or a section of music, "Try it again, but this time take off your boxing gloves."

If you mentioned any famous person to Pete, instead of him saying, "I'm a fan of his," he would invariably say, "Oh! He's a fan of mine."

On more than one occasion, when **The Jordainaires**, who sang background on many of Pete's artists' records, were in the recording studio, Pete would go out in the studio and hold his hand out in front of Ray Walker (the group's leader).

Ray would invariably give Pete the change that he had been jangling in his pocket, which was being picked up by the microphone and heard by everyone in the control booth.

Pete always kept his studio "loose," and almost anyone and everyone who is anyone would come by at night and see who was recording. His nocturnal visitors ranged from Waylon Jennings to Dolly Parton to Leon Russell. Dick Clark often used Pete's studio to record commercials and promotion "spots."

Pete Drake was a great teacher of the younger studio musicians and on more than one occasion gave them their *first gigs* in Nashville.

Hargus "Pig" Robbins, a blind studio keyboard musician was one of Pete's favorites. During a recording session, while the other musicians were writing out their charts, Pete would take a piece of paper, punch holes in it with a pencil, give it to "Pig" and tell him that he had written his Braille chart for him. I doubt if you can find anyone in Nashville who could say anything negative about Pete Drake.

George Hamilton IV

One night Pete called me into his office and asked if I would take George Hamilton IV out to eat. George Hamilton IV is known for his hit song *Rose And A Baby Ruth* and is a member of the Grand Ole Opry. I have been a fan of George's since I heard his recording of an obscure song called *Changes* on a jukebox in Meridian, Mississippi in the 60s.

Pete had subsequently scheduled two meetings at the same time and asked George if he could meet with him later. Pete's other appointment was with Chip Taylor. Chip is the writer of Merrilee Rush's and Juice Newton's mega-hit songs *Angel Of The Morning* and *Wild Thing,* recorded by the English group, The Troggs.

Chip Taylor is also the brother of Jon Voigt, the actor. Chip told the story about how his last name really is "Voigt" but changed it to become a songwriter. Jon kept the family name and became an actor.

Anyway, Pete gave me his credit card and George and I, dressed in our best blue jeans and flannel shirts, headed downtown to eat. The first place we came to was MARIO'S. Mario's is a five-star restaurant, and the Maitre De frowns at persons standing outside his establishment with blue jeans and flannel shirts. He curtly told us that there were no tables available (although when we looked inside, dust was gathering on some empty tables from lack of use).

Just as we were about to leave, Terry Bradshaw and Jerry Crutchfield, who were dining near the door, saw us. (Terry Bradshaw is the former quarterback for the Pittsburgh Steelers; is in the NFL Hall of Fame, and owns four Super Bowl Rings. Jerry Crutchfield is a famous record producer with credits for recording artists such as Tanya Tucker and Lee Greenwood.) Jerry got up and told the Maitre De that George Hamilton IV and I would be joining them at their table.

Suddenly, George Hamilton IV and I became "somebody" at MARIO'S five-star Restaurant.

Chapter 3

"Kink" And "Handsome" Harlan ...

At Pete Drake Publishing, Larry Kingston was the senior writer and one of the coolest guys that ever walked. He had a soft laugh and no idea you brought to the table was too foreign for him to try and co-write with you and make a song out of it. Larry and I must have written twenty-five or thirty songs together. On one occasion we were writing a song called *Three Ring Circus,* and Harlan Sanders kept popping his head in the door and saying, "I really like that song."

About the third time Harlan told us how much he liked the song, I looked at "Kink" (that was Kingston's nickname) and he looked at me, and we said to Harlan, "Come on in and help us finish writing it."

There was no jealousy or animosity among the three of us. We kept each other laughing too much to even think in those terms.

As a songwriter, Larry Kingston stood tall with the best. He had songs recorded by The Kendalls, Reba McIntyre, Porter Wagoner, Dolly Parton, George Jones, Vern Gosdin, David Allan Coe, Ed Bruce, Don Williams, Mark Chesnutt, Roy Clark—*Thank God and Greyhound You're Gone*, Jerry Lee Lewis, Ringo Starr, and many more. George Jones and Tammy Wynette scored radio exposure for their revamp of the Larry Kingston-Glenn Sutton song *Pair Of Old Sneakers* from one of their duets originally recorded by The Kendalls.

I'm proud to say that Larry and I wrote what is said to be Boxcar Willie's biggest Billboard Magazine chart song, *I Never Was The Man I Used To Be.*

Larry had been a recording artist for Warner Brothers Record label and had one of the smoothest country singing voices ever. All of our demos (with Kink singing) sounded like full-blown records. The only reason, I reckoned, that he didn't make it big as an artist was he was much too nice a guy and didn't seem to have a killer instinct when it came to the business part of the music. There's a saying in Nashville that "Music Business" is two words. I loved the Music part but despised some of the Business practices that were intertwined in our craft.

Chapter 4

Harlan Sanders...

That Goose would have made some good eating...

NOTE: When ducks and geese mate, it isn't always a pleasant sight. Sometimes they will get in the water and the male duck or goose will attack the female duck or goose's head and peck almost all the feathers off her head. The female duck or goose will, in turn, do the same to the male. This goes on during the mating ritual, and if you didn't know better, you'd think they were trying to kill one another.

Harlan Sanders told me that he owed his songwriting career as well as his freedom to Johnny Cash. Johnny Cash was playing a concert behind the walls of Folsom Prison when he met two inmates who wrote songs and somehow got his attention. One was Glen Shirley, who received more notoriety in the annals of *The Man in Black*, and the other was Harlan Sanders. Glen Shirley and Harlan Sanders were doing "hard" time in prison. Johnny pulled some big "strings" and both were released into his custody.

Johnny gave Glen and Harlan a staff-writing job for his famous House of Cash publishing companies. He gave them a "draw" (advance against future earnings from their songwriting) of fifty dollars per week.

Harlan said that the fifty dollars didn't go too far, and more times than not, by the end of the week they wound up broke and hungry and dependent on their girlfriends to bring them something to eat and drink at the cabins on Old Hickory Lake that Johnny Cash had provided rent-free for them to live in.

Harlan liked to tell the story about the time all the guys in the cabin were out of money and were waiting for their girlfriends to bring them something to eat, but the day was getting late and the girls hadn't shown up yet. He said the guys in his cabin were hungry, and everybody knows that hungry men will do almost anything to get fed.

There were some ducks and Canadian Geese that frequented Old Hickory Lake during their migration route south for the winter, and Harlan said on that particular day the yard in the front of the cabin was full of them (ducks and geese). They finally arrived at a plan where Harlan and his friends would catch a goose and cook and eat it.

According to Harlan, the geese, although wild by nature, had been around humans so long that they would walk right up to anyone who had breadcrumbs or anything that resembled something to eat. (I've witnessed this myself.).

Well, they finally caught one of the geese and couldn't figure out a way to kill it. Harlan said there was a garbage disposal in their cabin, so they decided they'd take the goose and stuff his head in the garbage disposal. Someone turned on the garbage disposal motor, and Harlan said he had the duty of holding the goose's head in the hole until it (the goose) expired. He then held the goose's head in the garbage disposal hole in the sink for less than a minute, and there came a knock on the door so he turned the goose loose.

At the door of the cabin were the girlfriends of the songwriters with sandwiches, beer, soft drinks, and cigarettes.

Harlan said the goose's bill was damaged somewhat, but otherwise it didn't seem to be hurt very badly and waddled out in the yard in front of the cabin to join the other ducks and geese.

Early the next morning, Harlan said he heard something making noise at the front door of the cabin. He then said when he opened the door and looked at eye-level there was nothing, but when he looked down there was the goose they had caught the day before—damaged beak and all—trying to get in their cabin.

Someone later explained to Harlan the mating rituals of ducks and geese, and Harlan reckoned that his goose had apparently fallen in love with the cabin's garbage disposal.

Handsome Harlan and my Sports Coat ...

Harlan Sanders was easily one of my favorite people. I have many favorites. Harlan stood about five feet-five inches but carried himself much taller. He had an infectious smile and would always greet you with these words, "Handsome Harlan here!"

There was always a wooden-tip Tampa Jewel cigar in the corner of his mouth, and it's hard to imagine him without it.

I'm about five feet-nine-inches tall, and when I first met Harlan he was about to receive a BMI Award for his George Jones song. He was in need of a sports coat to wear to the BMI Banquet. He asked me if I had a coat he could wear. I told him "yes," but that the discrepancy in our height might be a problem. He came over to our house to pick up my coat, and when he tried it on, the coat was so big it almost swallowed him. I was in some kind of shock, because Harlan carried himself so tall that in my perception of him, compared to myself, Harlan was a giant, and I actually thought he was taller than I. This is a true story.

Harlan had success as a songwriter and as a recording artist. He was signed to the CBS Label, and on one of his album covers is a picture of Harlan dressed like a cowboy and riding a milk cow with a saddle on it.

Harlan's mega-hit song *If Drinking Don't Kill Me—Her Memory Will,* co-written with Rick Beresford, was a # 1 country hit by George Jones. Other artists who recorded Harlan's songs are Ed Bruce *If It Was Easy.* Harlan, Larry Kingston, and I wrote many songs together, and each one was an experience in laughter.

I got a letter a few years ago from Rose Drake saying Harlan had passed away. I really miss him.

Chapter 5

Larry Henley And The Squirrel In The Margarita...

Larry Henley is in the Songwriter's Hall of Fame. He is probably best known for co-writing with Jeff Silbar, the Grammy Award winning song and Song of The Year, *Wind Beneath My Wings*. Some of Larry's other hit songs were *Till I Get It Right,* a number one song for Tammy Wynette and the "B" side of Kenny Rogers mega-hit *Lucille,* co-written with Red Lane, *Precious Are The Few,* co-written with Jeff Raymond and Lathan Hudson. It wasn't uncommon for writers from different publishing companies to co-write with one another.

Larry was also the lead singer in a '60s group called **The Newbeats**. He sang the high soprano part in the hit song *I Like Bread And Butter; I Like Toast And Jam.* A popular saying was that Larry Henley *could sing as high as a goose could fly.*

One evening a bunch of us songwriters were gathered at our favorite watering hole. We were swapping jokes, telling stories, and just having a normal creative evening. Some of us were drinking beer, but the specialty of the place was *fishbowl* margaritas. They were called that because the glass they were served in was as big as a small fishbowl.

It was summertime and we were sitting outside on the pavilion under the trees and were listening to Larry tell some of the funny stories of which he had a never-ending supply.

He said he had hitchhiked through the Arizona desert once and had caught a ride with a beautiful brunette in a small foreign sports car. She had given him her name and phone number, but he had lost it. Larry said he reckoned it must have fallen out of his billfold when he took it out and offered to pay for her gasoline for the trip through the desert. She refused to let him, however.

Larry then said that on the way through the desert, the brunette had swerved her sports car and had almost avoided a collision with a large jackrabbit. The rabbit was stunned in the accident, and she immediately got out of the car and took an aerosol spray can from her purse, held the rabbit up by his ears and sprayed him thoroughly. As she drove away, Larry said he looked back and the jackrabbit was standing on his hind legs and was making a circular motion with his forepaw, and that he did this until they were out of sight. When he asked the beautiful brunette what was in the aerosol can that she had sprayed on the jackrabbit, she said that it was *permanent wave for damaged hare.*

No sooner than he had gotten the story's punch line out of his mouth, a squirrel that had been playing in the tree above us lost his footing and fell—I swear—square into Larry's *fishbowl* margarita. He landed so perfectly that the glass didn't tip over immediately. It just sat upright for a few seconds and then spilled in slow motion. The squirrel stood on the table and shook himself off like a wet dog, hopped down on Larry's thigh, shook himself off again, then scampered up the tree.

Things were real quiet for a few seconds because no one could believe what had just happened. Then Larry reached up, scratched his ear, and said nonchalantly in his high-pitched voice, "You know! You just don't get quite as much squirrel in your margarita as you used to."

Squirrel in the Margarita

Chapter 6

"Ol" Tom Wopat And Me...

I had been a player for the Warner Bros. Softball team in 1977-78 and our shirts had the *WB Bugs Bunny* logo on the front with the number on the back. I read in the newspaper one day where there was to be a "reading" or audition in downtown Nashville for acting roles in an upcoming television *pilot.* The plot was supposed to be about two fun-loving "good ole boys" in a country town. The show, which could conceivably become a series, was yet untitled.

The paper said anyone could show up and "read" for an acting part, or role. I got the directions and the reading was to be held at a suite in a downtown hotel. Warner Brothers was holding the auditions. I wore my Warner Brothers softball shirt to the audition.

The lady who was conducting the auditions was late in arriving. I walked in the room full of people and noticed that everyone was staring at my Warner Brothers shirt.

I looked around the room, stood up, and in my best acting voice announced, "The auditions have been called off until next week. Please look in the paper for the new times."

The people in the room looked me over for a few minutes and then all but a small handful of non-believers left the building.

When the lady from Warner Brothers came in to do the audition, she said she expected more people than this would show up. Several people pointed at me and told her what I had done and said. She laughed, and when I read for a part, she kept my picture, phone number, etc. She told me that I might be good for a bit part in the series. She also told me she was glad I did what I did, because these things hardly ever amounted to anything and it was some kind of a SAG (Screen Actors Guild) law that they hold open auditions but, again, always a lot of wasted time on her part. I never got a call.

The pilot was a success and the television series became THE DUKES OF HAZZARD. John Schneider, one of the "Duke" brothers in the series, became a country singer and had a few hit records. Later, when Tom Wopat, the other "Duke" brother, became a country singer for the

Warner Brothers record label, I ended up coaching him on our softball team. Tom and I became good buddies, and he was one of our son's television heroes. Tom used to tell me that I was the *best third baseman he'd ever seen ... for an old man.*

Chapter 7

Red Lane Is A Myth...

L-R Frank Knapp, Red Lane, Billy Ray Reynolds, Lathan Hudson at Flora-Bama 1986

Red Lane is the most enigmatic person anybody ever met. Born Hollis Rudolph Delaughter (pronounced *Dee-Lawter*), in Bogalusa, Louisiana, Red had been an airplane Mechanic in the U.S. Air Force. Red always had the gift of songwriting and was a master guitar player.

Red went to see Justin Tubb perform in 1964 in Louisville, Kentucky, played him some songs backstage, and Tubb suggested putting them on tape and sending them to Buddy Killen at Tree. Killen signed Red to an exclusive songwriting deal after hearing the tape.

I first met Red right after I was signed to a staff-writing job at Tree Publishing. Red had purchased a discarded DC-8 airplane at an air field in Donelson, Tennessee and, to make a long story short (or a short story long), Red hired some house movers to cut the wings and the tail section off the airplane and haul it 40 miles (at night via Interstates 65 and 24) to Ashland City. There the plane was reassembled, and Red calls his DC-8 his "*Home Sweet Home.*"

Under one gigantic wing is his J-3 Piper Cub airplane, and under the other wing is his carport. There is so much insulation in the plane that the saying goes, "You can heat it with a candle and air-condition it with an ice cube."

The seats and all the wiring were ripped out of it and the motors were taken off the plane and sold for parts. I think Red said he purchased it for ten thousand dollars. I don't know how much he paid to have it moved. There is a bar and music room in the cockpit, and he has all of his taping and recording equipment there. It's set up to look like an airplane instrument panel. The pilot's yoke (steering wheel) is intact, and Red even had an original pilot seat installed. At night when the instrument panel (tape equipment) is lighted up, it looks like the plane could actually take-off.

Katie Hudson standing near Red Lane's DC-8 Home

Red is the most laid-back man in Nashville and can "out-quiet" anybody in the world. The good-natured jokes and sayings about Red are in abundance, i.e., "The first thing Red does in the morning when he awakens is take a nap" ... "Red is so laid-back that his younger brother is older than he is" ... "It takes Red 24 hours to watch 60 Minutes." Don Gant said it best, "Red doesn't do anything, because he doesn't have time."

The fun part about Red's airplane was to go to Ashland City and build a big fire beside the plane, cook a big pot of beans, drink beer, and have guitar pulls all night long. A bunch of songwriters would leave the Tree building and would invariably meet at Red's airplane, and from that point, the party was on.

Red was such a prolific guitar player that Chet Atkins signed him to the RCA record label as a singer. He said, "Chet didn't even ask me if I could sing—I guess he just figured I could." Red scored a minor hit song with his, Johnny Slate, and Larry Henley's composition, *The World Needs A Melody.* They were later sued because the song had a *release line* using the words and melody of the famous gospel song *In The Sweet Bye And Bye.* Red and Larry assumed that the song, *In The Sweet Bye And Bye,* was in Public Domain but found out the hard way that the song's copyright was still in effect.

Red Lane

Red played lead guitar for Merle Haggard and co-wrote songs with him. Merle recorded more than thirty-five Red Lane compositions. Red told a story about when he was on the road as "lead" guitar player with Merle. He said they were playing in Cleveland, Ohio, and the bus had just pulled into the motel where they would be staying. The Merle Haggard show was scheduled for the next night, so Red and some of the musicians decided they'd go downtown and see the sights.

Red went into this club by himself. The marquee read: **Appearing Nightly: RED LANE**. Red said he just had to check out the show, and onstage was a good looking guy, singing, playing guitar, and calling himself Red Lane. Red said that Red (the entertainer) knew every one of his—the real Red Lane's—songs and put on a first-class show.

36

I asked Red if he confronted the bogus Red Lane after the show and told him who he was. Red said, "Heck no, Hoss! They love me in Cleveland, Ohio."

Chapter 8

Darrel And Willie...

During the 80s, Darrel Royal and Willie Nelson held an annual golf tournament every spring in Houston, Texas. Darrel Royal is the former University of Texas Head Football Coach and loves country music as much, or more, than anyone I've ever met. Willie Nelson was/is Darrel's best friend, and they often travel to Willie's concerts together on Willie's bus.

The golf tournament is sponsored by the Boy Scouts Of America, and the monies raised go to the United Way charity. The tournament is set up where songwriters are invited to play golf as *celebrities* and many wealthy Texans and people of stature from other states pay for the privilege of playing golf and hanging out with *celebrity songwriters* (to me, that always seemed like an oxymoron). Anyway, each night for a solid week there would be a banquet in the big clubhouse. (The years I attended, the tournament was held at The Woodlands Country Club in Houston.) After dinner each night, there would be a "guest" recording artist in concert. Each night after the concert, the songwriters would meet in the loft of the clubhouse with their guitars and sit around the room and play songs for Darrel Royal.

Coach and his Whistle...

Everyone called Darrel Royal Coach, and he would sit in a chair in the middle of the room and, while a songwriter was singing his song, if anyone in the room talked, Coach would blow his whistle and whoever was caught talking while a song was being played was asked to leave the room for the night. Coach really loved his country music.

I had been signed to Tree Publishing as a staff writer for only a few weeks, and Sonny Throckmorton and most of the other Tree writers knew of my passion for football. At the time I didn't know about their connection with Darrel Royal or had no idea of his love for country music. One evening I was at the Tree building with the normal gang, or as Sonny liked to say, *the usual suspects.* Sonny asked me if

Coach Royal and his Texas Longhorns

I'd like to go with a bunch of the songwriters to Coach's for an all night bar-b-cue and some pickin' and singin'. My wife's parents were visiting us at the time so I called home and asked my wife, Katie, if it would be okay if I went over to Coach's and played some music and attend his bar-b-cue. I told her I would probably be gone for the night, because Sonny had said it would be an *all-nighter.* She said "sure" and told me to be careful and have a good time.

Not knowing what was going on, or even where Coach lived, I got in the car with Sonny and the other writers and we headed towards the airport. I thought maybe Coach lived out that way. We got to Nashville's executive airport, and there was a 10-seater Jettstar airplane on the tarmac with its motors running. We climbed aboard the airplane, buckled in, and were in the air in a matter of minutes. The plane belonged to then Texas senator Peyton McKnight.

We landed on a private airstrip in Austin, Texas, and there was a shuttle bus waiting to pick us up and take us to Coach's ranch. When we got to Coach's ranch, I had my first meeting with Darrel Royal and his wife Edith. I had been a big fan of Darrel Royal and, needless to say, I was speechless and in Hog Heaven at the same time. Coach and Edith are wonderful, down-home people. I bent his ear about everything I ever knew or thought about concerning the game of football.

Coach was holding a bar-b-cue bash for the University of Texas football team, and they had whole sides of beef on giant bar-b-cue spits. I learned that night that true Texans bar-b-cue beef and not pork. The food was delicious, and the company was even better. We took turns playing songs for Coach, the football team, and all of his guests, and then were shuttled the next morning back to the airstrip, climbed aboard the airplane, and flew back to Nashville. I found out later that Sonny Throckmorton's connection and Bruce Channel's connection was an old friendship that had been bonded with music, and both Sonny and Bruce were native Texans.

When I got home, my wife, Katie, asked if I had a good time at Coach's last night. I took her by the arm and said, "Darling, sit down. I have a story to tell."

Chapter 9

James Garner, "Rockford & Maverick"...

Red Lane was the primary reason I was ever invited to the Darrel Royal/ Willie Nelson golf tournament. At the time, I was signed to Pete Drake's publishing company and Red, Gloria Thomas (wife of BJ Thomas), and I had written some songs together that BJ had recorded. I mentioned that BJ had a worldwide #1 hit song on *New Looks From An Old Lover,* and for a while there Red and I were writing a lot of songs together.

Pete Drake's wife, Rose, ran the Drake Music Publishing companies, and was in essence my *boss.* Rose and Red were old friends, and Red asked Rose if their company would pay for my airplane ticket to Houston for the Darrel Royal/ Willie Nelson golf tournament. Red said he could get me an invitation, and all other expenses would be paid. Red convinced Rose that it would be good public relations, because I would meet a lot of songwriters that I didn't know, and we could conceivably become co-writers and do some business together. Rose said the company would pay for my airfare.

I don't like to fly on airplanes, especially big ones, and I prepared myself with a couple of vodka martinis. In the middle of the third martini, I was ready to fly the plane myself.

We got to the Houston airport, and a shuttle-bus was waiting to pick us up and take us to the Woodlands Country Club. Everything was first-class, and I spent one of the best weeks of my life just hanging out with music, movie and television celebrities, and all the other songwriters. I played some golf and met some of Texas' wealthiest men and women.

We stayed in these spacious bungalows that were located on and around the golf course. If I bought a drink or something to eat, all I had to do was sign a ticket and it was taken care of. It was brutally hot that particular week and during one round of golf, I went back to the clubhouse to cool off and didn't play the rest of the day. I met this couple, and we talked and had meals and drinks. I can't remember their names, but when I offered to sign the ticket to pay for our dinner, the husband said that he would take care of it. I told him that all I had to do was sign a ticket and the meal and drinks would be paid. He was insistent, and his wife grabbed my arm and said, "Honey, let him pick up the check. He's one of the wealthiest men in Texas, and we don't want to make him mad now, do we?" Stuff like that went on all week, and I forged some lasting friendships that are priceless.

Some of the other celebrities at the tournament were James Garner, Phil Harris, Jimmy Dean, football player/actor Terry Bradshaw, baseball "great" Mickey Mantle, football player Earl Campbell, the actor/singer "Scatman" Crothers. I spent an entire night shooting pool with "Scatman." Towards the end of our night, a lady who had been watching us shoot pool nervously went up to "Scatman" and asked him for his autograph.

She said, "I've seen every movie you've ever made, and I'm your biggest fan." She started naming off movies, both television and the big screen movies like THE SHINING ... SILVERSTREAK ... PAPERCHASE ... ROOTS ... DEATHTRAP, etc. When "Scatman" signed her autograph, she took the paper and said, "I'll never forget this night, and I'll never forget you—SCOUTMAN."

As she walked away "Scatman" turned to me and said in his best stereotypical black southern voice, "Lawdy mighty, Mr. Lathan, the Chile didn't even knows my name."

We both laughed until our sides hurt.

There were other celebrities there I can't recall.

James Garner came up to me and said there would be a guitar pull in his bungalow that night. He knew I was with Red Lane, and he gave me the number of his room and emphatically told me to tell Red *to be there*. Red and I showed up, and in James Garner's room was a Who's Who of country music songwriters. **Whitey Schaefer** *All My Exes Live in Texas* ... **Mickey Newbury** *American Trilogy, I Just Dropped In To See What Condition My Condition Was In*, ... **Glen Martin** *Is Anybody Going To San Antonio*, just to name a few.

James Garner told Red that he was to be the first singer and put a chair in the middle of the room for him. He then mockingly admonished Red for not coming to visit him on his ranch while he (James Garner) and his wife were temporarily separated. (Red later told me that he did spend some time with James once, but said, "After you said 'hi' to everyone out there in Hollywood, there wasn't anything else to talk about"). Vintage Red Lane.

Red had been a student of self-hypnosis and could put himself to sleep anywhere, anytime. He has his own wry, deep-seated sense of humor, and he sat in the chair that James Garner had provided, took his guitar and made a "D" chord and fell fast asleep. Everyone in the room was astounded. I wasn't, because I had spent about as much time with Red Lane as anyone and knew him pretty well.

Glen Martin took the guitar out of Red's hand and pulled up a chair beside him and, while Red slept, everyone in the room took turns playing guitar and singing new songs for James Garner.

I was sitting at a table next to Garner, and when Red finally woke up James told him it was his (Red's) turn to play a song. Red and I had just finished writing an inspirational song called *The Owner Of The Store Is Coming Back,* that BJ Thomas later recorded, and Red decided he would perform our song. Red doesn't like to admit that he co-writes. Although everybody knows that he does (like everyone else in Nashville), Red has a hard time giving credit to his co-writers. Red also has a hard time remembering lyrics to his songs.

Red then announced that he was going to sing a song that he had just written. Then he turned and our eyes met and he cleared his throat and said, "… er … uh, Lathan over there came up with the idea for the song."

I wasn't offended that he hadn't given me more credit for the co-write because, knowing Red, that was the best that he could do, and then he started singing the song. About halfway through his performance, Red forgot the lyrics. His face turned redder than it normally was, and then he got a mad look and turned to me and said, "Hey, Hoss, help me with the lyrics ... "

I turned to Garner, then back to Red and said, "Hell, you wrote the song—I just had the idea for it."

James Garner fell out of his chair and rolled over and over in the floor from laughter. Red just sat there getting redder and redder.

Newbury and laryngitis…

The night had grown into the wee hours of the following morning, and the guitar had been passed around many times. Each time it passed Mickey Newbury, he would whisper an apology and pass the guitar on to the next writer.

Mickey Newbury couldn't sing because he had developed a severe case of laryngitis, and it was killing him because he wanted so badly to try out some new songs he had written on what could easily have been the greatest group of songwriters ever assembled in one small room. Finally Mickey couldn't take it any longer, and he grabbed the guitar and announced to the audience that he would "mouth" the lyrics to his newest song. I don't remember what Mickey sung—or rather, whispered—but, when he got through with his latest composition, a feather hitting the floor would have sounded like someone banging a Chinese Gong in an empty Cathedral. Every writer and listener just shook their heads at what may have been one of the greatest performances of all time. I'm serious.

Once in an interview, Elvis Presley said in a ringing endorsement to Newbury's talents that he (Elvis) would *walk barefoot through a mile of broken glass* to hear Mickey sing.

The first time I met Mickey Newbury was in 1977 during a Writer's Night at the Exit Inn in Nashville. There is a room separate from the building in back of the performance hall where—during a writer's night—subsequent performers gather to tune their guitars, smoke, or just generally shoot-the-bull until they are called to play. I introduced myself to Mickey and told him what a fan I was of his. I didn't see him again until that night in Jim Garner's bungalow at the guitar pull. I walked over to shake his hand, and he looked at me and said, *"Exit Inn. Right?"*

I was full of myself for the rest of the night that he would remember a novice songwriter such as me.

The last time I saw Mickey Newbury was in 1986 at a Writers' Week in Flora-Bama. Me and Frank Knapp rode with Red Lane to Joe Gilchrist's establishment, which is a night club that stretched out into the Gulf of Mexico on the Florida-Alabama line—thus, the name *Flora-Bama*. I guess Night Club would be a misnomer because, even though part of it *was* a night club (one of the 21st century hurricanes literally blew it away), the owner, Joe Gilchrist, loves songwriters and songwriting so much that he devotes a large room strictly for songwriting, and during Writers' Nights, waiters and waitresses are instructed *not* to take drink or food orders while the writer is performing. Anyway, I walked out on Joe's back porch. There lying real still and wrapped in a sleeping bag was what I thought was a dead body. The sleeping bag and the head sticking out of the sleeping bag was covered with sand. Mickey Newbury opened one eye and said to me (almost apologetically), "We've been fishing all night."

We lost Mickey to Emphysema in September 2002. The music world's loss is Heaven's musical gain. Mickey was such a gentle spirit. One of my fondest wishes is to see and hear him perform at some Glorious Celestial Venue where we all hope to go someday.

Release The Condor ...

James Garner is one of the quietest people you will ever be around. Ironically, instead of his being so quiet you feel ill at ease, he puts you at *great* ease with his persona—I don't know how he does it, but after meeting him, he has the gift of making you feel like a long-lost cousin. I wish I was like that. He told a story to the gang of people who were gathered in his bungalow one night about some investors who wanted to start a Motion Picture Company and asked if he would participate.

James said the investment group wanted to call their company CONDOR PICTURES. They had somehow illegally raided a California Condor's nest and raised the baby Condor from an egg. They gave it the best of care and kept it in a pen and fed it the best feed or whatever it is you feed baby California Condors.

When the Condor was about fifteen months old and it came time to shoot the film sequences for the CONDOR PICTURES Logo, they took cameras, camera men, and the whole movie crew up on top of this high mountain. The idea for their identification logo was to release the bird and as it flew from the mountaintop (hopefully) in large circles the cameras would capture the scenes from all angles, and their logo would be complete, and the Condor would live happily ever after high in the mountains of California.

According to James Garner, the Condor was resting peacefully in his cage and as the director was getting ready to start the filming, he put his megaphone to his mouth and yelled, "Release The Condor!!!" The handlers shook the cage, and the Condor edged nervously to the door. The door of the cage was on the precipice (ledge) of this big mountain, and as the Condor was prodded from the cage, instead of flying in large graceful circles, he tumbled down from the mountaintop all the way to the valley below to his fate.

It seems that no one had bothered to ask if the Condor could fly. As a matter of record, the Condor had been raised in the cage it was in and had never been given the chance to learn the fine art of flying. He said that the investors figured that all birds could fly, and it (flying) should have come naturally.

The investors put out the word that "… the less said about the incident, the better … ," and it was years before the real story came to light. However, a common phrase was born from the incident, which a lot of people outside the film industry didn't understand. James said that when an actor or actress flubbed his or her lines repeatedly, or when a scene was messed up to the point of not being able to shoot it, someone in the filming crew would invariably say or yell, *Release The Condor!!*

Chapter 10

Red Lane at Thirty Thousand Feet...

On the plane ride back from Houston to Nashville, Willie Nelson had given Red a copy of his new record album. Red had written one of Willie's early hit songs called *Blackjack County Chain,* and Red and Willie were great friends. I think Red had a song on Willie's new album, and he had it in his lap. I was sitting directly across the aisle from Red. Red looks like a character right out of a Western Movie. He has long flowing reddish-brown hair, moustache and beard. He wears a cowboy hat and actually carries his clothes on trips in custom-made saddlebags. I was wearing a pair of slacks, loafers with no socks and a velour shirt.

The stewardess (they were called "Stewardesses" back then) came over to Red and knelt down, and they started talking about Willie's record album (which Red had in his lap). I couldn't resist, so I tapped the stewardess on the shoulder and said, "Ma'am, is that man a movie star?"

She turned her back more to me than before, and I tapped her on the shoulder again and said, "Ma'am, do you think I could get his autograph?"

She turned to me and said icily, "Sir! We don't bother passengers on this plane!"

She turned back to Red, and a minute or so later I tapped her on the shoulder and said, "Ma'am! I know he's a movie star or somebody. All I want is an autograph."

She stood up and put one hand on the back of my seat and said, "Sir! If you continue to pester this passenger, I'll have you removed from this airplane!!"

She was angry, and we were at 30,000 feet. Red started laughing, and I guess the stewardess picked up on the fact that we were together. She went to the back of the plane, and we never saw her again. Red looked over at me and said, "Hoss! You sure know how to run 'em off."

Chapter 11

BJ and Gloria Thomas ...

BJ Thomas' professional music career began in 1965 with a cover of Hank Williams' hit song, *I'm So Lonesome I Could Cry.* He followed it up a few years later with Burt Bacharach's and Hal David's Academy Award-winning *Raindrops Keep Falling On My Head,* which was featured in the movie BUTCH CASSIDY AND THE SUNDANCE KID. After a great career of pop songs which included *Hey, Won't You Play Another Somebody Done Somebody Wrong Song ... Eyes Of A New York Woman ... I Just Can't Help Believing (This Time The Girl Is Gonna Stay) ... Hooked On A Feeling* and many others, BJ decided to make his way into the Gospel and then subsequently, the Country Music market. BJ had signed a production deal with Pete Drake and they had great success recording Grammy and Dove Award-winning gospel albums.

Lathan Hudson, Thomas "Hollywood" Henderson, Pete Drake,
Gloria & BJ Thomas 1980

BJ's wife, Gloria, who is a very gifted songwriter and also authors children's books, co-authored many of these songs. She slipped out of the realm of writing children's books once and wrote a book about her and BJ's life and their conversion into Christianity called *In Tune—Finding How Good Life Can Be.* Even the title of Gloria's book became a Grammy Award nominated song co-written with Larry Kingston and me.

BJ says he will never stop recording Gospel songs, but in the early '80s, he decided to get back into popular music and into the country music mainstream. They (Pete and BJ) defined his music as *secular,* meaning BJ would only sing country songs that didn't have references to "cheating," "drinking" or "cursing." Even with *that,* some of his gospel fans deserted him and even though he recorded as many gospel albums as he did *secular* ones, the gospel awards abruptly ceased. BJ Thomas is his own person and stuck to his guns and figured that people are people and he would continue to be BJ Thomas.

BJ and Gloria Thomas commuted to Nashville from Arlington, Texas and owned another home in Franklin, Tennessee. BJ has a passion for golf and when he was in town recording, it wasn't unusual for BJ, his brother Jerry, and me to play three or four rounds of golf per week. Add that to the fact that I was playing four to five softball games per week at night, I was burning the candle, as they say, *at both ends.* My normal week day would begin by meeting BJ and his brother Jerry Thomas at a local golf course and play eighteen and sometimes thirty-six holes of golf, go back to the studio and meet with my co-writers about songs to write or status of songs written, go home, get my softball uniform, gloves, and shoes; go over to Pete Drake's house and sit in his hot tub until the soreness left my body, go play one or two softball games, then go back to Pete's house and sit in his hot tub and go home from there. I am fortunate to have a loving, understanding wife. Many marriages have met their end due to the subtle intricacies of country music.

I got a phone call once from Arlington, Texas. It was Gloria Thomas, and she and BJ were getting ready to make the trip to Nashville for BJ to record. She told me that she had a song idea that came from a happening at their home. Gloria said BJ was walking down the stairs and she had never seen him look so at ease, and she just fell more and more in love with him. She said her idea for the song was *I'm getting a new look from my old man.* I told her I thought the idea was great and when she got to town that we would attempt to write it, and would she mind if I asked Red Lane to help us with the idea? She said that would be fine.

It's funny how a seed can become a flower and just as strange how a seed of an idea can develop into a full-blown song. Gloria, Red, and I took her idea and twisted it around a few times until the hook-line and the title became *I'm Getting New Looks From An Old Lover Again.*

BJ recorded our song with Pete Drake producing, and the title of the album became *NEW LOOKS*. Although a song can be a title of an album, that is no guarantee that it will be a single record, or as they say in the business a *single*. The first single released off the album was a great song written by Lewis Anderson, *What Ever Happened To Old Fashioned Love*. Don Gant was the song's publisher and earlier in the year he asked me if I would play the demo for BJ. I almost got in trouble with Pete Drake because Pete said he didn't want to record a song on BJ with the feel of BJ's song *Raindrops Keep Falling On My Head* .... *Old Fashioned Love* had the same loping feel as *Raindrops* .... I asked BJ to promise that he wouldn't tell Pete I played the song for him, and it was much later, after the song became a #1 Hit that I confessed to playing the song for BJ. Pete was very forgiving.

Thank You, Conway Twitty...

The song *New Looks From An Old Lover* was never intended to be a single, because right after the success of *Whatever Happened To Old Fashioned Love,* Pete Drake put out the call to find new songs as he was preparing to record a new album on BJ. That meant that the *New Looks* album would have one single and the rest of the songs would be album cuts.

BJ was scheduled to sing two songs on a country made-for-television "Special" called "The Ernest Tubb Tribute." Many country music performing friends of Ernest Tubb were paying homage to the great *E.T.* and the "Special" was filmed in several segments and on many separate nights. The night BJ was supposed to sing his two songs, Conway Twitty was standing in the wings of the stage at the Civic Auditorium in downtown Nashville with Gloria Thomas and me. Conway was to be the next performer.

BJ's first song was his first big hit *I'm So Lonesome I Could Cry* and, probably because of the business part of performing a song of which you own one-third of the publishing and one-third of the writing (Gloria's one-third writing and their one-third publishing)—also, owing to the fact that the show would be in syndication which would garner a lot of airplay and would make a lot of money for the writers and publishers—BJ followed *I'm So Lonesome I Could Cry* with *New Looks From An Old Lover.*

When BJ came off the stage, Conway Twitty immediately asked him where he found that song, *New Looks.* BJ told him that his wife Gloria, Red Lane and I wrote it. Conway then said to BJ, "If you'll give me that song, I'll call my musicians together *tonight,* and I'll record it and *New Looks* will be my new single.

BJ countered with, "I'm glad you like the song, Conway, but that's going to be my next single. "

I guess sometimes it takes a voice in the wilderness to bring great things to light.

Thank you, Conway Twitty.

Chapter 12

The Indomitable Stan Byrd…

When I first met Stan Byrd, he was the head of Warner Brothers Records promotion department. The chief duty of promotion people in the music business is to "track" records to find out which radio stations are playing them. When songs are recorded and *singles* are chosen for each artist on the label's *roster*, the records are sent out by the promotional staff of each record company to radio stations throughout the nation. The initial phone calls are made to make the stations aware of the new single that has been shipped to their station and to ask the station manager at the radio station if they will "go on" (play) their song. Follow-up phone calls are then made to each station—called "tracking"—to find out if the stations initially called are indeed playing their record.

Since each station has its own individual "chart," the promotional staff of each record label—after finding out if their song is being played—indexes the chart position of each station called to get a true reading of how many times their songs are being played on different stations in each twenty-four hour period. To make a long story short, this is the way chart positions are determined in musical periodicals such as Billboard Magazine, Cashbox Magazine, The Gavin Report, and R&R Magazine.

Stan Byrd is also a gifted athlete and went to Texas A&M University on a basketball scholarship. Stan put together the first softball teams at Warner Brothers, and I ended up coaching one of the teams and played second base for the other. Stan later came to play for PETE'S FREAKS, a team sponsored by Pete Drake which I coached.

Stan eventually left Warner Brothers to start his own independent promotion company called ***Chart Attack Promotions***. He hired a staff to assist him and pretty soon, because of prior connections and the many thousands of calls made to radio stations throughout the country, his company became very successful.

Since all record companies have their own promotional

departments, it isn't unusual for some production and publishing companies like Pete Drake Music to hire independent promotion companies like Chart Attack. They do this for many different reasons. Sometimes the promotional companies of record labels aren't able initially to convince the radio stations to play their song. Independent companies such as Chart Attack are then called upon and are invaluable, because sometimes, something as seemingly insignificant as a favor done in the past, a friendship, or the respect a radio station manager has for someone like Stan Byrd, can be the determining factor and the difference in getting a song played on that station or not. This can have a monumental effect on the *shelf-life* of a record.

That being said, during the chart life of the BJ Thomas song *New Looks From An Old Lover,* when it reached number *fourteen* on the Billboard Chart, the promotional department from CBS (BJ Thomas' Record Label) called Pete Drake and said it looked like the song had pretty much *run its course* and was going to lose its *bullet.* They didn't expect it to go any higher than number *twelve.*

Pete Drake, having a long friendship with Stan Byrd, called Chart Attack Promotions (Stan's company), and asked Stan if he would "go on" the record. A deal was struck between Stan and Pete, and the staff at Chart Attack started making calls to the stations that weren't very keen on the record.

Ironically, BJ Thomas and Stan Byrd are both from Texas. Also, it's ironic that BJ wasn't getting much play from the country stations in Texas. I can only surmise that every station manager regarded BJ as a "pop" artist. They wondered *why was he trying to become a staple in the country market?*

Stan Byrd has clout...

Under normal circumstances, Stan would have his staff make the calls to the stations that weren't on BJ Thomas' record *New Looks From An Old Lover.* In this instance, however, Stan got on the phone to the music directors of the biggest Texas stations and started pulling in favors and telling them that they were making a mistake by not "going on" the song. Eventually they did. *New Looks From An Old Lover* took some of the biggest jumps in the history of Billboard Magazines. In four short weeks *New Looks From An Old Lover* climbed from *fourteen* to *thirteen* … and from *thirteen* to *seven*—then to *number one*.

The Ronnie Milsap song *Don't You Know How Much I Love You* was positioned at *number two* and was ready to go to *number one*, but stayed at *number two* an extra two weeks, because *New Looks From An Old Lover* jumped from *number seven* over the Ronnie Milsap song to *number one*.

Thank you Stan Byrd and Chart Attack. And Stan, you were one heck of a softball player.

Chapter 13

"Hollywood" Goes Nashville ...

When I first moved to Nashville, there was a saying that "Nashville was about forty years behind Hollywood." I like to think that at least in one instance, "Hollywood" came to Nashville.

On one of BJ Thomas' trips to Nashville to record with Pete Drake producing, he brought Thomas "Hollywood" Henderson with him. BJ was in the process of helping "Hollywood" kick a drug habit that had gotten him in a lot of trouble and subsequently gotten him kicked out of professional football.

Thomas "Hollywood" Henderson was one of the best linebackers that ever played the game and maybe the fastest. He played his entire professional career with the Dallas Cowboys and wore a Super Bowl Ring.

Thomas "Hollywood" Henderson was a fun-loving, intelligent man with a glib tongue. Once, to Terry Bradshaw (then all-world quarterback for the Pittsburgh Steelers), "Hollywood" said, "Terry, you couldn't spell Cat if someone spotted you the 'C' and the 'T'."

That hit a sore spot with Terry, and he has never forgotten it.

BJ asked me to "baby sit" with "Hollywood" while he was recording at Pete Drake's studio. Somehow, that night, Red Lane joined us, and Thomas showed us a song he had written. The "song" was about six pages long and told the story about how sometimes friends and teammates will desert you in a time of need. Essentially, his song was—according to Thomas—about how Preston and "Too Tall" had screwed him.

Seems that Coach Landry had come to "Hollywood," Preston Pearson, and "Too Tall" Jones (Preston and "Too Tall" were also star players on the team), and said he knew that they were doing drugs, but the Cowboys couldn't afford to kick all three off the team and someone would have to *take the fall*. Preston Pearson had some towels manufactured for sale with the "#1" logo on them. Since "Hollywood" was already in Landry's doghouse for waving Pearson's #1 towel in a game when they were getting beat real bad, "Too Tall" and Pearson pointed to "Hollywood." Landry kicked "Hollywood" off the team.

Red Lane said there was a song idea in "Hollywood's" story and with a little rewriting, the three of us came up with a song that was somewhat *less* than six pages long. We titled the song *Friends* and BJ Thomas recorded it the very next night. Some of the lyrics are:

> *... It's never lonely at the top*
> *friends keep coming, they never stop*
> *try to find one when you're down*
> *they don't come around*
> *none that you can really call your friends*
> *talking 'bout real friends*
> *stronger than a sister/brother*
> *glad to die for one another...friends.*

Tomorrow I'll Sing It Perfect ...

BJ, Jerry Thomas, Red Lane, and I were playing golf the day after BJ recorded our song, *Friends.* BJ turned to me and Red and said, "I rushed through the lyrics on your song. Tomorrow I'll go in and sing it perfect."

I said, "Please, BJ. Please don't touch that song. It *is* perfect."

BJ laughed and said, "No, tomorrow, I'll sing it perfect."

I don't know if you understand the significance of what BJ was saying. He was not boasting, or being vain. BJ's measure of his singing is "perfect," and he uses the word like you and I would casually ask someone for directions. Man!!!!

Hollywood had the last laugh because a few years ago he won 25 million dollars in the Texas lottery and is now devoted to his ministry against drugs. He is drug-free and doing very well with his charities.

The last time I talked to "Hollywood" was before he kicked his habit. He called me from an Oklahoma prison and was telling me how drugs had messed him up and was actually preaching to me.

I wish I could pass my collection plate to him now.

56

Chapter 14

Co-writing with Pete Drake...

During the time Pete Drake was producing BJ Thomas, it was a common practice for songwriters to conveniently visit Pete more than the norm and " ... just happen to have a song with them that might be good for BJ." Red Lane was the exception. He hardly ever showed up anywhere unless he was invited.

One night I went up to Pete's office, and there was Red and Pete. Red had his guitar and Pete had a pen and writing pad. I had never perceived Pete to be anything other than a great musician and record producer and made some comment like. " ... didn't know the *Drake-Man* could write."

He laughed and said, "Help us write this song."

Pete said he had had an idea for a song for a long time and didn't really have time to work on it. He had called Red and asked him if he would come over and work on the song with him, and now they were inviting me. I was, and am, honored to have my name on a song with two music "giants" like Pete Drake and Red Lane.

Pete's song idea and the title (after we finished it) was *You Keep The Man In Me Happy—And The Child In Me Alive*. The song tells of unconditional, undying love and devotion throughout a couple's childhood, courtship, and marriage. BJ Thomas recorded it the following night. It came out on the "B" side of the then 45rpm single record *New Looks From An Old Lover* when songs were recorded on vinyl.

There used to be an old music saying, *if it ain't vinyl—it ain't final*. I guess with the advent of CDs and whatever will come next, that saying has gone the way of the dinosaur.

Coughing Up A Song

Red Lane and I scheduled a meeting at Pete's office the next night to write. I guess we were burned-out from the night before, because we must have sat and stared at one another for thirty minutes without a single idea worth writing crossing our minds.

I had just gotten over a bout of the flu and had this dry, hacking cough. Every twenty seconds or so, I would make this low, disturbing hacking sound with my cough. Try as I may to suppress it, I could tell that it was getting on Red's nerves. It was getting on my nerves, too. I guess the pressure of two "professionals" like ourselves not being able to come up with a single song idea was too much, because Red blurted out, "Hey Hoss! Don't be coughing on me!"

I explained to Red that I had read in a physician's periodical (I made that part up for Red's benefit) that the flu germ dies after 48 hours of your first getting sick, and the good antibodies continue to fight one another long after the bad antibodies have died—and that, even though the cough lingers, essentially, the bad antibodies had done *all the damage they could do* to me.

Red looked me in the eye and proclaimed, "Hoss! There's our song idea!"

We then proceeded to write the song *When We've Done All The Damage We Can Do.* Louise Mandrell and her then husband R.C. Bannon recorded the song a week later as a duet. The song was featured on their album titled *You're My Superwoman/ You're My Incredible Man.*

I laughingly tell everyone that to date the song that Red and I "coughed up" has sold well "under" a million copies.

Chapter 15

Red Lane—Professional Dreamer...

The year was 1979, and we were living in an apartment in the town of Hermitage near Percy Priest Lake. Our son Hud was twelve years old and was actually a fishing guide on the lake. Hermitage was then a sleepy town about ten miles from Nashville and was a perfect place for us because of the recreation the lake afforded. One of Hud's first customers as a fishing guide was Kix Brooks (of Brooks & Dunn) and Kix's father.

Segue to Hud's fishing story ...

As I said, our son, whose nickname is "Hud," was about 14 but had been a fishing guide since he was 12 years old on Percy Priest Lake in Hermitage, Tennessee. The older men who we referred to as *Old Geezers* that hung out around the dock used to make fun of Hud's homemade boat that he and I built out of an old boat hull we had bought from Hall of Fame Songwriter Sonny Throckmorton.

One day before a fishing trip, we went to the seafood section of a local supermarket, and I bought three or four small (ocean) Red Snappers, one (ocean) Grouper, and a medium-sized (ocean, of course) Lobster.

We put them in his *Live Well* in the boat. (All were dead, and we bought them frozen, naturally.) After we came in from fishing—sure enough—The Old Geezers were waiting to make fun of Hud and asked him what he caught. Hud said he caught some Red Snappers and Groupers. The laughter got real loud and they began to yell, "Hud, show us your fish! Show us those Monsters!"

When Hud held up his stringer of fish, you could have heard a pin drop. I really don't think they've figured it out to this day. One old man finally got up enough nerve to ask Hud what he had been fishing with?

"Hud" Hudson in his handcrafted fishing boat.

A movie screen writer couldn't have scripted this scene any better. Hud held up a medium-sized Lobster and answered, "Crawfish!" I don't remember the Old Geezers ever bothering Hud again.

Red Lane—Semi-professional Sleeper ...

Red Lane lived part time with Hank Cochran about twenty miles from us, and the Tree Publishing Company was a halfway point for us to meet. (Actually, Red was renting a big farmhouse from legendary songwriter Hank Cochran at the time.) On this particular day, however, Red called me from Hank's house and said, "Hey Hoss, get over here and let's write a song."

I got in my car and drove the twenty miles to Red's house, and when I walked in, he was sitting behind this big desk strumming his Martin guitar.

I grabbed a writing pad and a ballpoint pen off the desk and sat back in this big chair across from Red. Without saying anything, Red strummed a "D" chord about two or three times on his Martin and fell fast asleep.

I eased up out of my chair, laid the pen and pad on the table, got back in my car, and drove the twenty miles back to our apartment. As soon as I walked in the house, the phone rang. I answered it, and of course, it was Red on the other end of the line.

He said in this high-pitched shrill voice that he uses sometimes for humor, "Hey Hoss—Where'd you go? I looked up and you were gone!"

I told him if he wanted to work on a song today that he'd have to come over to our place and write.

About an hour later, Red pulled up in our parking lot. He brought his guitar in, took it out of the case, and we drank a couple of cups of coffee. Red then stretched out on our couch, fell asleep, and slept the rest of the day. He spent three days and nights with us. The only time I remember him getting off the couch was to go to the bathroom, grab a sandwich and a soft drink, or take a shower. My wife Kathy is cool. She just did her housework around him like he was a piece of furniture. We may have left a song or two in Red's guitar case during that time.

Cold, Cold Kentucky and Red Lane on the Juke Box
(It's hard to say if this story belongs here, but here goes.)

I was working construction up in Kentucky while trying to break into music. The year was 1979. It was the coldest winter in Kentucky in 70 years, and I was digging footers with a backhoe for Hardaway Construction Company out of Nashville, Tennessee. We were building a Casket Factory for Bates Casket Factory of Ohio.

Like I said, it was miserably cold and, although I had had some minor success as a songwriter, my music "monies" hadn't quite gotten to the point where I could support my family on it, and I had to follow my "day" job (construction) wherever it would lead me.

Pretty soon winter turned to spring, and the job was coming along, and I had gotten to know a bunch of Kentuckians. Kentuckians are no strangers to partying, and we did party a lot on our off days.

On one particular occasion, I had gotten an invitation to one worker's house for a party. It was a Saturday night, and I had bragged to everyone I worked with that I had come to Nashville to be a songwriter, and before long they would be reading about me. I was in line for fame and fortune.

The party was in full swing, and I had consumed my fair share of beer and Vodka. The guy who owned the house where the party was being held had a juke-box in his house with his favorite collection of old and current .45 rpm country records. I was reading the list of songs on his jukebox, and wouldn't you know it? There was a song on there called *The World Needs A Melody.* Not only was the song co-written by my friend Red Lane, it was Red's RCA recording of the song.

I called the owner of the house over to his jukebox and told him—in a loud voice where everyone could hear—that Red Lane was one of my best friends and that Red and I had written several songs together. In retrospect, this was not about to become my finest hour.

The owner/host looked at me and his fun-loving attitude became very dour. He said in a very threatening tone, "I hate it when people try to be something they're not by saying they know somebody famous!"

I thought for a minute, started for the door, and said in a loud voice where everyone in the room (which had gotten quiet and solemn because—due to my earlier prompting—everyone at the party had been listening), "I never heard of Red Lane in my life—I don't know what you're talking about, and that's the truth!"

Chapter 16

Paul Craft And His Small Dog ...

Paul Craft has a gift of making almost anybody laugh. I really don't think he realizes it when he is being funny, but he is definitely one funny person. It's hard to make Paul laugh. I am one of the few people who can lay claim to that distinction (of making Paul Craft laugh).

Paul is the writer of some of the funniest songs ever heard. His *It's Me Again Margaret* (a song about an obscene phone caller who keeps calling the same lady even after he is arrested) is one of Ray Steven's most popular recorded songs made into video. Paul had a minor hit on the same song in the early 70s.

Paul Craft is one of four songwriters to have two solely-written songs nominated for a Grammy in the Best Country Song category in the same year (1977). The songs were *Dropkick Me, Jesus (through the goal posts of life)* and *Hank Williams, You Wrote My Life*. Given the amount of co-written songs coming out of Nashville and music in general, that statistic will probably stick around for a while.

His song *Midnight Flyer* was included on an Eagles album, "On the Border," and Paul's *Keep Me From Blowing Away* was part of Linda Ronstadt's album, "Heart Like a Wheel," in 1975. Paul played guitar on his Linda Ronstadt song.

Paul recorded a self-penned album with songs like *Linda Lovelace, Come Sit On My Face, And I'll Do The Same For you ... She's My Bedroom Woman, I'm Her Living Room Man* and *Elvis Was A Narc*.

I had been a fan of Paul's, but had never met him. In the early 70s, a buddy of mine and I spent about two dollars worth of quarters playing his song *It's Me Again Margaret* on a juke-box in Birmingham so we could include it in our show during my barroom music days.

After we moved to Nashville, I got a call from this guy who said he had just recorded my George Jones song *Leaving Love All Over The Place*, and he said his name was Paul Craft. I actually spent time trying to convince him that he wasn't Paul Craft, and that I was a

Paul Craft fan, and that his joke (telling me that he was Paul Craft) was in bad taste. He finally convinced me—through a mutual friend, Beckie Foster—that he really was Paul Craft and that Chet Atkins had produced my song on him on RCA Records. I was flabbergasted. Had Elvis Presley called me, I really don't think he would have had as much impact as when Paul Craft called me. Honest.

We used to go to this *listening room* called "Mississippi Whiskers" to hear Paul play. He did a one-man show, accompanying himself on guitar. Paul stood almost motionless (except for his hands and mouth) and looked almost exactly like Chevy Chase, the comedian/movie actor. He hardly ever smiled, but told these absurd stories and sang the funniest songs you'll ever hear. Part of his show was a *give-away bag* of assorted gifts. For no particular reason, this one skit he did always kept me laughing uncontrollably. Paul would hold up a small cloth dog with straw stuffing coming out of his side and say in deadpan seriousness, "We have here—a 'small dog.'" I would invariably have to go outside to catch my breath from laughing so hard. You almost had to be there.

Earlier, I said I had once made Paul laugh. Every time I talk to him, he reminds me of it. Here's the story:

I had pitched a song to a record producer named Norris Wilson. His nickname was "Norro."

I thought my song was a perfect "pitch" to his then current artist (I can't remember her name). When "Norro" turned my song down—for some unexplainable reason—I was fuming, because I had written this song for this particular artist and had never felt a more perfect song "fit."

I played my song for Paul Craft. and he volunteered (without my prompting) that it would be a perfect "pitch" to this particular artist and asked me if I had pitched it to "Norro" Wilson for his artist and had "Norro" heard my song?

I looked at Paul for a minute and Paul asked again, "Has "Norro" heard your song?"

I looked at Paul real hard and emphatically said, "**Norro Wilson couldn't hear a train coming!!**

For some reason, that struck a funny nerve in Paul, and he laughed so hard that I thought he was going to have a coronary. He said it was the funniest thing he had ever heard and (again) still reminds me of it every time I see or talk to him ... *I guess you had to be there.*

Note:
I emailed Paul Craft the rough draft of the segment I wrote on him, and he emailed me back. This is the unfettered email that Paul sent to me ...

Lathan ...

I'm flattered!!!! Some stuff you might want to know: Waylon (Jennings) and (Johnny) Cash recorded *"Keep Me From Blowing Away,"* but neither one has been released. I heard the Cash version, and he said, "I'm a back-slidin' Christian" in his version, which I stole and use now when I sing it.

Waylon sang the wrong tune and made it sound like a steal from *Ole Five and Dimers,* which it wasn't. Willie just recorded it on some sessions produced by Buddy Cannon and Kenny Chesney. I had played it for Buddy and for Kenny, but had heard that he might do something with Willie so .... whatever it takes.

The thing I used to take out of the bag was a "young sheep" and that was funny. *"Elvis Was a Narc"* was written by Lewis Anderson and Fred Koller. Lewis and I got to talk to Jay Leno about the song and other things at a restaurant one time. I also had a little Jimmy Carter doll and when you punched down on his head his little *pookie* came out from under his skirt, and it was a peanut.

As I remember, what you said was, "He (Norro Wilson) can't hear a train comin'."

I'm gonna send you some stuff that you'll like. Great to hear from you.

I'm sending a copy of this to my son so he will possibly know that guys like me (and you) did something beside sit around on our butts. We did, didn't we??

Kix (Brooks) has done alright, hasn't he?

Paul

Chapter 17

Roger Miller And Airplanes...

Roger Miller

Sometimes irony is layered so thick you can't even cut it with a knife. I had only met Roger Miller two or three times, and each time was an experience in zaniness. I was at Tree Publishing one day and walked into the office of Dan Wilson. Dan was Tree's song "plugger," a person who is normally hired by a music publishing company to play songs for prospective artists to record. Roger Miller, Bobby Braddock, Don Cook, and Dan were in the office. Roger was being Roger, and everyone was laughing.

I had never formally met Roger Miller, and I shook his hand and told him I was one of his biggest fans, but that his biggest fan lived in Butler, Alabama. His name was Joe Knight. I had worked in a paper mill in south Alabama with Joe in the mid sixties. I told Roger that Joe knew every song Roger Miller ever recorded and had even gotten into a fistfight with a paper mill worker who had argued that Hank Williams was a better songwriter than Roger Miller.

Rogers reply was, "Well Lathan, you just can't tell how fat a chicken is by looking him in the face, can you?"

I reckoned you couldn't.

How's this for a segue? Roger laughed and began to tell a story about airplanes.

To preface Roger's story, we were living in Georgia in the late sixties, and Roger Miller was a guest on the Merv Griffith talk show. He had a guitar and sat in the chair next to the host (Merv Griffith) and played a song called *The Day I Jumped Out Of Uncle Harvey's Plane*. Ironically—and I didn't know it at the time—the song was written by Red Lane.

The big sport going around Nashville at the time I met Roger Miller was parachuting. Almost every male at Tree Publishing—and even some of their wives and girlfriends—had parachuted.

Please remember that that was before "tandem" parachute jumping. Personally, I adhere to the adage, "Why jump out of a perfectly good airplane?" Personally, I don't even care to climb into a perfectly good airplane.

Roger proceeded to tell his story. He said someone had talked him into parachuting. His parachute was strapped on his back, the plane was in the air, and everyone except the pilot and Roger had "left" the plane and were floating to the ground. Roger said he stood in the open door of the plane and just couldn't bring himself to do it.

The pilot then walked back to where Roger was, stood behind him and said, "Roger, I've put the plane on auto-pilot. I want you to know that I'm gay, and if you don't get out of this plane, I'm going to pull your pants down and have my way with you."

Bobby Braddock, who was aghast at the story, asked, "Roger, did you jump? Did you jump?"

Roger said, "Well, Bobby, I did a little bit—at first."

That was vintage Roger Miller.

Roger Miller, Larry Henley, And The Small Dog ...

One of our favorite "watering" holes was a little restaurant/ tavern called The Third Coast. I guess it got its name because Nashville has sometimes been referred to as "The Third Coast." California is the West Coast … New York is the East Coast …you get it.

Anyway, most of us liked to meet there at the end of the day and sit outside under the big Oak trees and pass the time relating the day's music happenings and telling stories that were true and/or almost-true. If I think back hard enough, we may have even enjoyed a beer or two—and sometimes something a bit stronger.

Roger Miller and Larry Henley were two of The Third Coast's most famous and favorite patrons for a short stretch of time, and everyone enjoyed listening to their stories. You could always spot the table where they were sitting. It was the loud one with hardly any empty seats.

Roger and Larry would work on telling funny stories by adding to their stories each time they met at The Third Coast. I don't remember the inception of the Small Dog story, but Larry blamed it on Roger, and Roger blamed it on Larry. We later allowed that there was probably no small dog named Rusty, the dog in their story.

Like I said, their story was told in layers; and in the end, I actually added to the story and put it in my first published book of fictional short stories called *Thurmond—Permanently Sealed.*

Roger Miller & Larry Henley take turns telling about their small dog Rusty ...

"The reason I haven't said a lot about my small dog, Rusty, is because of the anguish it brings me each time I think of him.

"The Prince of Whales gave Rusty to me when he was just a pup. No! Not the 'Prince of *Wales'*—the 'Prince of *Whales!'* You know—that fellow that feeds all those sea animals down in Miami, Florida.

"Anyway, I brought Rusty home and trained him to do normal tricks like *fetch the stick, roll over,* and *shake hands.* I trained him with a dog whistle I had carved out of an old lightning-struck Dogwood tree (naturally). The secret was, the whistle only blew bass notes.

"Rusty was a natural when it came to squirrel hunting. I'd take him out in the woods, and he would look up and sniff the air until he came to a tree where he thought there was a squirrel. Then he would bark and, sure enough, there'd be a squirrel up in that tree. I was so proud of Rusty.

"Well, one day I was out in the pasture bush-hogging, you know, clearing some land with my tractor. I really thought Rusty was in the house watching *Lassie* or some other show on TV. Anyway, Rusty ran out in front of my tractor and right under my bush-hogging blades. By the time I stopped the tractor and got to Rusty, he was lying there with all four of his legs missing.

"I wrapped him in my shirt and rushed him to the veterinarian. Of course, the vet wanted to put Rusty to sleep, but considering all that we'd been through together, I asked him if there was an alternative. He told me that he could sew up what was left of Rusty's legs (leaving little more than dimples attached to his body). I told him that any part of Rusty was better than no Rusty at all, and so sew he did.

"I took Rusty home and although rehabilitation was slow, I did manage to teach him new tricks like *how not to fetch the stick*, and how to *roll over...and over...and over,* and *how never—no matter how tempting—to shake hands.*

... Sometimes with Roger telling the story, sometimes with Larry

"I thought Rusty was going through a normal period of depression until I realized that what he really missed were the squirrel hunting trips we used to go on. So, I got this old wheelbarrow out of my garage and threw some blankets in it and placed Rusty on his back and together we headed for some deep woods located on farmer Doug's farm. Farmer Doug told us that we could hunt his woods, but it was important that we come out before dark because of the woods being so deep we could easily get lost. I told farmer Doug I understood, and off we went. The Hunting trip was very successful. Rusty would bark, and I would locate the squirrel hiding among the branches in the tall trees. We were having a ball.

"Time passed, and it became morning—and we're still in the woods. As we're coming out of farmer Doug's deep wood—me pushing the wheelbarrow with Rusty still lying on his back and looking very content—I look down and my clothes are shredded from running through the briars and the brambles. Then, I notice blood coming from scratches on my arms and legs. As we near the edge of the woods, I hear a familiar, *'Hall-o-o-o!'* from Farmer Doug.

"Well, as we cross the clearing to where Farmer Doug is standing, he says, *'I told you you'd get lost in the woods if you let the sun go down on you!'* I explained that we didn't get lost. What happened was, we were coming out of the woods with plenty of daylight left when this gray fox runs out in front of our wheelbarrow, so me and Rusty chased him all night long.

"The story could end right here, but there's more …

"It's mid-July, and it's hot! Rusty is in front of the TV watching re-runs of *Lassie* or some other show, and I have to go into town.

"I get in my car and turn the ignition key and nothing happens. Then, I go back into the house and look through my morning newspaper and read where the local auto parts store is having a sale on battery jumper cables. And—get this—if you buy your jumper cables before five o'clock you get, at no extra charge, a free set of *wooden dog legs*! Man! I can't pass up a deal like this, and I get there a good ten minutes before the sale ends.

"I was very fortunate because when I bought my jumper cables, I also got the last set of size small *wooden dog legs* in the whole store. And, with Rusty being the small Terrier that he was, I was on top of the world.

"The *wooden dog legs* were a perfect fit, and was Rusty ever happy! First, he ran round and round in the front yard. Then he ran around in the back yard. He did have some problems, however, trying to dig up some bones that he had buried there before the accident.

"This is the sad part … it hadn't rained for two months, and the weeds were tall and dry near the road where Rusty was playing. Anyway, a car came down the road and the driver threw a lit cigar out the window. And with the weeds being so dry and all, it started a brush fire which caused his little wooden dog legs to flame up and burned my little dog Rusty to the ground."

Chapter 18

John Anderson and Lionel Delmore

John Anderson and Lionel Delmore will surely someday be in the songwriters Hall of Fame. (It should have already happened.) John Anderson will someday receive the accolades he so richly deserves as a recording artist by being inducted into the Country Music Hall of Fame.

In 1978-79, John had just signed with Warner Brothers Records as a fledgling recording artist. He and Lionel Delmore were inseparable and co-wrote most of John's songs. The string of hits Lionel wrote with John included: *It Ain't Pneumonia, It's the Blues, ... I Wish I Could Write You a Song ... They Spent Forever ...* and *Bad Weather.* But the song they may be most remembered for is *Swingin,* which topped both the country and pop Billboard charts in 1983 and was named the CMA Song of the Year.

Lionel was the son of Alton Delmore, one-half of the Delmore Brothers of Grand Ole Opry fame, Elkmont, Alabama natives elected to the Country Music Hall of Fame October, 2006. The duo wrote such classics as *Browns Ferry Blues ... Beautiful Brown Eyes ... Midnight Special ...* and *Blues Stay Away From Me.*

I coached John Anderson in softball for the Warner Brothers team. He had an infectious laugh and "nobody" didn't like John Anderson.

John and Lionel in the a.m.—story number one ...

Aside from his being fun to be around, two stories will forever be embedded in my mind each time I think of John. One of them involves Lionel Delmore and the other story doesn't.

After each softball game, it wasn't an uncommon thing for most of the team to find the closest tavern to whichever softball field we happened to be playing on that night and recap the game over some "suds" and discuss other various-and-sundry things.

Some of the players would crowd around a pinball machine if there was one, and some of the players' girlfriends and/or wives would be sitting at the table with us and, for the most part, and most of the time, we were a pretty tame bunch. I'll get back to that thought later.

On several occasions, we would have a brew or two too many, and the player who had drunk the least amount of beer would drive some of the others home. Lionel and John had my phone number, and sometimes my phone would ring around 2:00 a.m., and it would be John and Lionel calling on the pretense that they were checking to see if I got home okay.

They lived together in an upstairs/downstairs duplex in a small suburb of Nashville called Antioch. John would be on the upstairs phone and Lionel would be on the downstairs phone and we'd end up talking about everything under the *soon-to-be-rising sun* to songwriting.

Lionel would say in his slow, southern drawl, "Lathan, you're a dang good songwriter, and it will just be a matter of time before you're one of the ones the record producers and artists will be chasing down for your songs."

John would concur.

Pretty soon I'd get so sleepy that I couldn't talk anymore and I'd hang up the phone without saying good-bye, good-night, or good-morning. The next time I'd see either Lionel, John, or both, they'd say, "Lathan, after you hung up the phone, we talked to one another (over the phone) till daylight."

We lost Lionel Delmore to cancer in 2002. One of my regrets is that I didn't co-write a song with Lionel and John Anderson. They were definitely two of my buddies, and I'm sure that could have been arranged had I the foresight to have made it happen.

It's a shame that Lionel will probably be inducted to the Songwriters Hall of Fame posthumously and not during his lifetime where he could have enjoyed the fame he so richly deserved.

John Anderson and Phil Jones—story number two ...

Phil Jones was one of the Warner Brothers Softball players. Phil was the Road Manager for Ronnie Milsap and was a great softball player. He stood 6'2" and weighed about 250 pounds. Phil was a former professional football player for the Buffalo Bills and the New York Jets and stayed in great shape.

On this particular night, we had played a softball game against the Nashville Police Softball Team. The irony of this story lies in the fact that Warner Brothers sponsored the police softball team.

As usual, we stopped at this tavern to discuss whatever we deemed important to discuss, and on that particular night Phil Jones had a few more beers than some of us.

For whatever reason, the waitress called the police to report that this softball team (Warner Brothers) was getting rowdy and needed to be calmed down. Two Nashville police squad cars with no less than eight policemen arrived and barged into the tavern with no intention of even asking what was wrong and started pushing the softball players up against the wall. At least half of these policemen were the same ones who had played against us that night in the Warner Brothers Police softball players versus the regular Warner Brothers softball team that I coached.

Instead of coming into the tavern and talking some sense with either me or Stan Byrd—who was one of our players and who was really in charge of buying the Warner Brothers uniforms and outfitting the police team—they chose to arbitrarily just barge in and begin to act like robotic idiots and begin what turned out to be a needless brawl where someone could have been severely injured.

Phil Jones was in the bathroom at the time and I really don't know for certain what happened except that a fight ensued with four policemen and Phil Jones. Trust me when I say that the *policemen* were severely outnumbered. They were swinging their night sticks and wrestling Phil's knees trying to get him to the floor. Phil was slinging the policemen all over the bathroom like they were rag dolls.

Two more squad cars arrived with the two K-9 German Shepard dogs on a leash. This is where it gets kind of funny, because the policemen finally had Phil subdued and had his hands cuffed behind his back. They then threw Phil in the back seat of one of the squad cars.

While they were standing around (remember now, there were at least 16 policemen and four or five Nashville Police squad cars on the premises) trying to get a report from the owner of the tavern (who later, incidentally, fired the waitress for calling the police), Phil Jones—6'2" and 250 pounds—was busy kicking the door off the squad car he was locked in and running into the woods behind the tavern.

On one of the K-9 handlers command to track down and attack Phil Jones, the well-trained German Shepard Police dog immediately attacked a lady who was walking across the parking lot to her car and bit her leg and her arm, requiring stitches and resulting in a lawsuit.

Later Phil told us what happened from his point-of-view. Here was Phil with his hands cuffed behind his back hiding in the woods behind the tavern. He said he wasn't sure if he was hid well enough, so he thought he'd run a little further into the woods. Instead of doing that, Phil had lost his sense of direction and ran right back into the parking lot where all of the squad cars and the policemen—with their German Shepard dogs—were waiting.

The K-9 dog handlers then gave the command (again) for the dogs to attack Phil. The last I saw of Phil that night, the dogs were trying to bite Phil, and Phil—with his hands cuffed behind his back— was face to face with one of the German Shepard dogs, making a growling, snarling noise, trying to bite the dog.

Phil said the policemen put him on the elevator at the jail and gave him the "...we'll-stop- the- elevator-between-floors ... " treatment, meaning that they beat Phil some more on the elevator with his hands tied behind his back. When I saw Phil the next day, his face was cut and badly bruised.

Phil Jones has a very wry sense of humor and told us that at his trial the Judge admonished him for beating up his poor policemen and sarcastically asked him how big he was? Phil said he answered, "Your Honor, I'm about 6'2" tall and weigh about 250 pounds. That's without a flashlight, a billy-club and a military pistol strapped to my side."

John Anderson had left our gathering earlier in the night and when he heard a partial story about what had happened, got a flashlight and went back to the tavern and began a search for Phil Jones.

I don't know why this part is so funny to me. Maybe it's in the way John tells the story—or, maybe knowing John, it's so visual to me—but John said he was walking around in the woods early in the a.m. with his flashlight looking for his friend and whispering nervously, "Phil! Phil! It's John! John Anderson! Phil! Phil! Phi ..."

Chapter 19

Angela Kaset, will you write a song with me ...?

I've often wondered why there is a second "a" in Angela's name, because Angela Kaset is an *Angel*. I have taken her a total of seven song ideas to co-write with me and never has she turned any of them (the ideas) down. Not only that, the songs we co-wrote were what is known as "top-drawer" quality. Percentage-wise, we are batting almost 1,000 in getting them recorded, and it's hard to do much better than that.

Angela is easy to write with, easy to be around, and so very, very talented. We were staff writers at TREE Publishing at the same time in 1978-79, but as fate would have it, didn't write with one another until well past our TREE days.

Angela was predestined to be a major recording artist with platinum records adorning her walls. At least, that's what everyone predicted at the time. However, knowing her the way I do now and knowing a little something about the politics of music—or, as they say, "Music's dark underbelly"—Angela kept to her rigid set of values and wouldn't succumb to some of the shortcuts that are in effect in almost every business. I'm not saying that everyone who is successful—especially women—take these shortcuts, but, like it or not, women are the most vulnerable and consequently, they *are* sometimes there for the taking. Angela was also focused on the way she wanted her music (as an artist and as a writer) to sound and hardly ever veered very far off her path.

She has been very successful as a writer and as a recording artist, but she definitely did it— and is still doing music—*her way.*

One of the first songs we wrote was called *The Man In The Moon Song.* I don't have any favorite Angela Kaset/ Lathan Hudson songs, but one of the most requested at some of our "guitar pulls" is *The Dollmaker.* Jim Ed Brown (re: an earlier part of the book) sang *The Dollmaker* to open and close his television series GOING OUR WAY. We also wrote Martin Delray's *Ring Around The Moon* with the late Johnny Cymbal (again, re: an earlier part of the book). Johnny wrote and had a hit song as an artist on *Mr. Bass Man* and was the writer of *Mary In The Morning* of Elvis Presley and Al Martino fame.

I think one of the best ecological songs I've ever been involved in writing was with Angela. The song is called *Mother's Garden* and tells of a Buffalo and a Crippled Old Eagle who meet to discuss how best to clean up the mess we've made of our Earth. Some of the lyrics are:

> *When the earth becomes green again*
> *And the rivers all run clean again*
> *When the trees in the forest reach for the sky*
> *Then Mother from her garden*
> *Will grant her children a pardon*
> *There'll be hope for us all*
> *The great and the small*
> *And a place for the Eagle to fly*

Angela's London Invasion...

Angela Kaset wrote *Something In Red,* A huge hit song for Lorrie Morgan, and recorded it herself on the Chrysalis Record Label. She was invited to London to play some songs live for BCC Radio Stations—she did some that she had co-written with two of my writers, Tom and Kenya Walker, who were SESAC writers, and they had to index them for the radio station log books.

I had applied to SESAC for the name **Cunning Linguist** to be my SESAC publishing company name, and although it is in close proximity to the word cunnilingus, I thought I could justify it by saying that it meant *a clever person of languages.* BCC Radio didn't think it was funny and told Angela so. As a matter of fact, she said they got belligerent with her.

Chapter 20

My Early Years In Music City…

Nashville has been called a *tough room* because, no matter how good you are at your craft of songwriting, unless you have made some connections and met the right people to play your songs for, you might as well be sitting in the middle of the ocean in a rubber life raft without oars or directions to shore.

The year was 1976. I had overcome some of the early obstacles, dodged a few land mines, had gotten my foot in some doors, and had met Lamar Morris. Lamar was managing Danny Davis' music publishing companies. Lamar was a big Cherokee Indian. He was also Hank Williams, Jr's brother-in-law. At the time Lamar was married to Lycrecia, Audrey Williams' daughter and Hank Williams' step-daughter, and had played lead guitar in Hank Jr's band. But at the time I met him, he had a part-time road gig playing lead guitar with a country group called BILLY THUNDERCOUD AND THE CHIEFTONES. Billy Thundercloud and his brothers were full-blooded Indians and were making some noise (no pun intended) in the industry at the time.

Lamar had a track record of writing great songs. He had co-written with Darrell McCall the hit song *Eleven Roses* recorded by Hank Williams Jr. *Eleven Roses* was unique in that it had only one verse and one chorus. It was the 1973 **Billboard magazine's Song of the Year**.

I actually met Lamar Morris in 1975 while we were living in Birmingham, Alabama and I was trying to make at least one or two trips per month to Nashville and find out as much as I could about the music life in Nashville and "would I really stand a chance of becoming a songwriter?"

It was at that time Lamar was playing on Mercury Record's softball team. For some reason, there was a softball game that day and somehow, he got me a Mercury Records jersey, loaned me a glove, and I ended up playing second base for the team. Jerry Kennedy was the player/manager and, as I have already mentioned, Jerry was the head of A&R (Artist & Repertoire) at Mercury Records.

I forget what team we were playing, but it was the bottom of the last inning and there were two outs. We were losing by one run and Jerry came to bat. I had been the lead-off hitter in the game and followed Jerry who was batting last. Anyway, being kind of cocky, I told Jerry that if he got on base, I would "bring-him-around" (get him home with the tying run).

Jerry got on first with a "walk," and there was no fence in right field . It sloped-off into some woods past where the right-fielder stood. Being a left-handed batter, somehow I jerked the ball down the right-field line past the right-fielder and I think— to this day—that the ball is still rolling.

Jerry scored the tying run and I came in right behind him with the winning run. Jerry is a large man. He is short, but stocky and weighed then about two-hundred-and-forty pounds. He grabbed me up and hugged me so tight that I couldn't breathe.

Lamar had told Jerry that I was a songwriter (one of the prerequisites for being on the team) and Jerry told me that if I ever had a song for any of his artists, for me to bring it to his office and he would personally listen to it. I immediately had an open door to one of Nashville's best record producers. Wow!

On nearly all of my Alabama/Nashville commutes, I would go by Lamar's office and bring him songs or sometimes just song ideas and if he wasn't busy, we would write them. Lamar was a great musician and would demo the songs on a portable multi-track tape recorder with him singing lead vocal, harmonies and playing all the instruments. Sometimes, if the song was either a duet or written for a female, he would hire an artist named Beckie Foster. Beckie had the voice—and the looks—of an angel and demoed my first "female" song. Our musical paths would cross many times during my tenure in Music City.

Lamar Morris was from Alabama and had a *good-ol-boy* sense of humor. Sometimes I would outline an idea for a song to him and often as not, the idea would be scrapped for something better, but he would always comment on it (the idea). Once I had this song idea with the hook line ... *And while you're sleeping, I'll be keeping my love warm for you.* The song would be about a man who worked nights and thought about his wife all during his working hours. The woman would naturally be singing the song with the above hook line. Lamar said tongue-in-cheek, *"During the night, maybe we could have her sliding down the banisters."* That idea was immediately scrapped.

Fan Fair ain't Fair anymore…

In the early seventies, one week out of the year was devoted to the fans of Country Music. It was usually the first week in June, and during that week, Country Music Fans reigned supreme; thus the name Fan Fair. They (fans) would literally come from all parts of the world and Nashville's population would increase that week by many thousands of people of all origin, shapes, and sizes. Hotels and motels were full, as well as campgrounds and RV Parks.

During that week, almost all of the Country Music Recording Artists would be in Nashville. They would purposely keep their working calendar "open" as the week where they wouldn't book any out-of-town gigs. Fan Fair Week was the week that the fans could literally rub-elbows with their favorite Country Music Singer or Music Group.

Being the 70s, a family could come to Nashville during Fan Fair Week and on a modest budget could go to the Civic Auditorium and see the major label shows and watch the best country music artists in the world perform. Then they could go to the municipal softball fields and watch some of the same artists, great songwriters and music business people play a two-day softball tournament for the record labels or publishing companies they represented with a huge trophy presentation on the final day for the winners. Everyone could walk out onto the field after the games and literally rub elbows and talk to the musicians and artists and get them to sign a *free* program with all the participants in it.

It isn't that way anymore. Now, it costs a fortune to go to the "package" shows and some of the recording artists have bodyguards and you can't get within thirty feet of them unless your Platinum Credit Card is visible. Tents are set up and the recording artists are stationed behind a barrier and to get an autograph you have to buy an expensive article with that artist's picture on it. Every event is corporate sponsored, and if they could find a way to charge for breathing the air, I'm sure they would. Money rules.

You're a little bitty thing ... Marty Robbins is a giant ...

Two years before we moved to Nashville, my wife, myself, and two friends of ours went to Nashville for the 1974 Fan Fair. It was our first trip to Nashville and we were wearing our matching country shirts and blue jeans. We were *country-come-to-the-city.* The show we attended featured CBS Records recording artists and our favorite was **Marty Robbins**. He was wearing a beautiful all-white suit with turquoise bracelets and necklace. On stage, Marty looked ten-foot tall.

After the show we rode down on Music Row to see all the major record companies buildings and the publishing houses. We hoped to catch a glimpse of someone famous walking the streets of Music Row.

Marty Robbins' company was called Mariposa Music, and as we drove by the building, Marty was getting out of his car and was still in the outfit in which he had performed a few hours prior.

I walked up to the door of the building, and Marty Robbins opened it and politely asked if there was anything he could do for us? I told him that our wives would like to have his autograph (I wanted one myself), and he said for me to tell them to get out of the car and come in. As Marty was introducing himself to us and my buddy and I were introducing our wives to Marty, my wife pointed at Marty and blurted out, *"You're a little Ol Bitty Thing."* My wife Katie was shocked at his diminutive stature—Marty Robbins is only about 5'4," and it was one of those embarrassing moments where you just want to hide and stick your head in the sand. Marty was taken aback by her shock, and all of a sudden he was on the defense and almost apologized for being of short stature.

He feebly said, "Well, er ... I've been sick and ..."

I tried to think of anything to say and interrupted with something like, *"To us, you're a Giant."*

Suddenly, the moment was smoothed over and we were all relieved.

I had brought a demo of the first song I ever wrote called *My Heart Belongs To The Wind* and asked Marty if I could play it for him. He was such a great person and congenial host to us and our interloping ways and put the reel-to-reel on his Wollensak tape recorder.

Marty commented on how well the song was written and asked us if we would like to hear his newest composition and what would eventually become his next big, big hit record.

Marty Robbins then played the song *El Paso City*. His new composition was a sequel or prequel to his smash hit *El Paso*. His new song was an eerie tale of a Cowboy flying over the city of El Paso at 30,000 feet in a commercial jet and somehow knowing that he was the reincarnate of the Cowboy in the song *El Paso*. It goes to relive the Cowboy's love for his long lost maiden *Feleena*. Not only could Marty Robbins sing a great song, he could write one as well.

I would like to mention that the occurrence of our being able to interact with a star of Marty Robbins' stature—and even play a song for him—was not an uncommon one at the time. However, almost any songwriter today who experienced the Nashville scene in the 60s and the early 70s will tell you emphatically that *those days are long gone*.

Lamar and I wrote a song ,*The Best Is Yet To Come* recorded by Johnny Duncan and produced by Billy Sherrill. The song was initially about a man and woman having a night on the town and ending up in a motel. Lamar took it to Billy Sherrill who produced all the great music on George Jones, Tammy Wynette, Joe Stampley, Janie Fricke, David Allen Coe, Johnny Paycheck and almost every act at CBS Records. Billy suggested as a surprise-ending verse, that we should have the couple "leaving the motel the next morning and going to their home where their children were waiting for them." In other words, a married couple having a *real* night on the town.

Lamar and I wrote three ending verses for the song and Billy chose the one that he felt would best fit the song and recorded it on Johnny Duncan, a hit artist at the time. The title of Johnny's album was our song, *The Best Is Yet To Come,* but was never chosen for a single.

I've often wondered, in today's frenetic music pace, how many times a busy famous record producer takes the time to help struggling writers with a song. I'd bet it happened more then than now.

Chapter 21

That's How I Got To Nashville ...

If you love somebody enough—you'll follow them wherever they go—that's how I got to Memphis—that's how I got to Memphis (Written by Tom T. Hall)

Although this book is about characters I either met or heard about in Nashville, it is important to me that I acknowledge some friends who were either directly, or indirectly, responsible for my getting to Music City.

There are no accidents ...

In 1975 I was living with my wife, Katie, and our ten year-old son, Hud, in Birmingham, Alabama. I had written maybe a total of five songs at the time. I had always wanted to be a songwriter, but had no idea where to go or what to do to be one. Everyone I played my songs for said they were good and I should send 'em in. I was ready to send 'em in. Problem was, I didn't know where to send 'em.

To make a living, in between heavy equipment operating jobs, I was painting apartments in the daytime for the landlord of the apartment community we lived in, and at night a buddy of mine, Ron Muir, and I were playing our guitars and singing songs as a duo at local nightclubs and bars around town. I also tended bar in one of the clubs three or four nights during the week.

Sometimes during the day, my buddy, Ron Muir, would come over to an apartment I was painting. He'd bring his guitar and sit on the floor, and while I painted he would play, and we'd either write a song or go over some songs we were going to add to our barroom repertoire.

Lathan Hudson

How many refrigerators does it take to check a wall plug?

On one particularly hot day the apartment landlord, Jim Hicks, interrupted my painting (and our rehearsing) and asked if Ron and I would be interested in making a few extra dollars by taking a new refrigerator up three flights of stairs to an apartment. Apparently, the tenant had called and said her refrigerator was broken and she needed a new one.

We put the new refrigerator on a "dolly" and pushed, pulled, tugged and sweated until we got the refrigerator up the stairs and into her apartment. We took the old refrigerator to the shop and went back to the upstairs apartment and plugged the new refrigerator in the wall socket. Nothing! Well, we took the new refrigerator down the three flights of stairs and back to the shop and got another new one. We took it up to the apartment and plugged it in. Nothing!

To make a short story long—after three new refrigerators and spending half the day tugging, pulling, pushing, and sweating over the seemingly faulty refrigerators—the lady who rented the apartment asked if we had checked the wall plug. We plugged a lamp into the wall plug where the refrigerator was supposed to be plugged in. Nothing! The wall plug was faulty.

The night of our next singing gig, we took turns asking the audience if they knew how many refrigerators "does it take" to check a wall plug? The answer is "three."

I was and still am a very average-to-poor guitar player but my buddy, Ron, was very good, and during our performances I would sit on his right and watch his hands for chord changes in the "cover" songs we were playing. We had a group of sympathetic friends who would follow us from club to club (bar to bar), and it was easy to find work because our fans usually made up more than enough in beer tabs to cover what we were being paid each night. It was a good deal for the clubs/bars … and for us.

There was the night a customer who had had one-too-many sat and watched all three of our "sets." We just knew we had a great fan because he nodded approval with each song and applauded regularly. When he got up to leave, he walked up to the stage where we were playing and said, "Guys, I want to say one thing. Every song you sing is better than the next one." We thanked him, then he left the bar.

Ron looked at me and asked if I heard what he said. I said, "Yes," and repeated it. Then I thought for a minute, and we both laughed and told the audience. That saying became a part of our act for the remainder of our barroom career.

At a venue called the FIFTH QUARTER, which was a steak house chain, Ron and I had talked the manager into letting us play in the bar. The FIFTH QUARTER had two eating rooms divided by a bar. On crowded nights, while waiting for a table, patrons would wait in the bar until their names were called to eat. The two rooms were the "MOSS BUCKET ROOM" and the "NATTY BUMPO ROOM." (I'm not making this up).

Ron Muir, my duo partner, and I shared the microphone with the lady who called out the names of the people whose tables were ready. For instance, she would say something to the effect, "*Table— party of four for James Spradley to the* MOSS BUCKET ROOM." Then, Mr. Spradley and his party of four would be led by a waiter to their table. Our "partner" would give us a signal (signifying a table was ready) and if we were in the middle of a song, we would immediately go into a "guitar vamp" and she would announce the table.

LAUGH-IN's Dick Martin ...

One Saturday night, during our FIFTH QUARTER gig, Ron and I were having our usual repartee with the audience. There was a party of four at a table right in front of us that seemed to be enjoying our music more than most. They gave us extra applause after our songs and laughed louder at our jokes than we were normally accustomed. Naturally, we played to the table and started making comments about how beautiful the two ladies were and much one of the gentlemen looked like Dick Martin of the then hit television series *Rowan & Martin's Laugh In*. We even started calling him Mr. Martin and made up our own *Laugh In* jokes as if he were really Dick Martin. He would then embarrassingly shake his head no when we'd ask and prod him for a reply. Everyone in the room, and especially couples at the table we were playing to were enjoying our fun and taking it good-naturedly.

Finally, it came time for the 'announcer' to give us a sign to do our guitar vamp while she called the patrons to be escorted to their dinner table. Her announcement went something like this: *Party of four for Mr. Dick Martin – to the* MOSS BUCKET ROOM.

It really was *Laugh-In's* DICK MARTIN. We found out later that he was in Birmingham on some business and after they had their meal, he and his party came and watched the rest of our show. I have to believe, and as near as I can remember, our jokes weren't quite as funny from then on because of our nervousness.

A "Chance" meeting ...

Before moving to Birmingham, we lived for three years in Dothan, Alabama and through an attorney friend, Herman Cobb, I had met a friend and college roommate of Herman's, Johnny "Chance" Jones, who is now one of my very best friends. "Chance" was living in Birmingham but had lived for a short time in Nashville and had some music contacts there. Chance was then an insurance adjustor, and his job wouldn't allow him to stay in Nashville to follow his dream of being a professional songwriter.

In spite of not living there, Chance has had good success as a songwriter because of his talent and his diligence. I wish I had his work ethic because he laboriously follows the songwriter's credo of *write ... rewrite ... then rewrite some more.* His songs are always excellent.

I've had the good fortune to be able to co-write with *Chance* Jones, and we had a cut by Tammy Wynette on a song titled *You're Kissing Me – All Over Again.* Ironically, Chance and I co-wrote it with Ron Muir, my old singing partner. The three of us also wrote a song called *The Jingle Bell Monster* recorded by Jon & Jim Hager of HEE HAW fame.

Kris Kristofferson, Larry Ezell & "Funky" Donnie Fritts ...

Larry Ezell would be proud to know that I used his name in one of this book's captioned segments in the same sentence line with Kris Kristofferson and "Funky" Donnie Fritts. Larry was then a golfing buddy of mine in Birmingham and told me he worked with a Nashville songwriter's uncle. I asked him who the songwriter was and he said, *"'Funky' Donnie Fritts."*

You could have blown me over with a feather. "Funky" Donnie tours and is the keyboard player for one of my all-time favorite songwriters, Kris Kristofferson. He is also one of Kris' best friends and plays in almost all the movies Kris makes. "Funky" Donnie played the part of *Beaver* in the movie PAT GARRETT & BILLY THE KID. Irony runs deep again—Bob Dylan, who swore his songs would never show up in commercials and/or movies, wrote the music score as well as the album. Bob Dylan also played in the movie.

Larry Ezell, David Van (one of my best friends from Dothan, Alabama who now lives in Birmingham), Moose Hill (Larry and David's brother-in-law), and our wives went to see Kris Kristofferson and his band perform when their tour brought them to the Civic Center in Birmingham. Through Larry Ezell's contact ("Funky" Donnie's Uncle Jack), we had dinner with the band after their performance, and I was in Hog-Heaven. Here I was sitting among my music heroes and probably didn't eat a bite of my food.

Through a series of events—especially, the one where I met "Funky" Donnie Fritts and Kris Kristofferson—I started making trips to Nashville with a few songs on tape and a *pocketful of dreams.* "Funky" Donnie got me an appointment with Kris and Donnie's publisher, Combine Music. The guy at the publishing company pretty much said the three songs I played for him *stunk*, but at least I found out that someone would listen to my songs and there'd be no stopping me from then on.

Interstate Highway 65 goes through Montgomery, Alabama, and goes through Birmingham and right on up to Nashville, Tennessee. Every time my wife and I would get in our car and drive out on I-65, we would pretend we were going to Nashville. I guess she got tired of pretending, because I came home from work one day, and she had the contents of our apartment packed up in cardboard boxes and said we were moving to Nashville. I said okay.

We moved to Nashville July 1st, 1976 and after we paid the deposits on our apartment and had the electricity turned on, we had a total of two-hundred dollars to our name—and I had no job. Thanks to my wife Kathy's mother and father, we had a freezer full of meat and one week's worth of groceries. Both our families were very supportive of our move.

Early in our marriage, I had worked as a heavy equipment operator and in Nashville found a job operating backhoes, bulldozers, and cranes with Hardaway Construction Company. That was perfect because on rainy days I could knock off work and spend my time pitching songs to publishers on Music Row. I was in Heaven.

We had a great friend, Jack Hare, from Birmingham, who was a principal at a local grammar school, and he would call my wife as a substitute teacher and that added immensely to our then meager income. Jack was also a performer/songwriter and one of the best tennis players ever. Jack passed away with anorexia nervosa at the age of 34. Jack was Chance Jones' best friend. For the short time my wife and I knew Jack, he was our best friend also, and we greatly miss him.

I'm sure every songwriter, singer or musician-in-general who ever made the trek to Nashville has a similar story. As the sayings go: "Someone has to do it," and "Everybody has to be somewhere," or "No matter where you go—there you are." I'm writing this from our Carriage House in Apalachicola, Florida, so I guess at this point in my life I can say, "Here I am."

Epilogue

The purpose for the "Volume 1" in the title of this book is that I intend to write a series of books with more stories I inadvertently left out of this one. The stories are literally never ending.

I honestly believe that Country Music is literally a Force—I believe that the Force is so strong and durable that no matter how many changes we put it through or how much we abuse it and/or try to reinvent it, Country Music has the power to heal itself.

Until that day, me and a bunch of good-ol-boys and good-ol-gals will be hanging out somewhere—waiting patiently ...

—The End—

Some "Tongue-in-Cheek" Musical Terminology

STUDIO: A building with sound-duplicating equipment where musicians and singers record songs

PITCHING A SONG: The act of playing a song to an artist or producer for recording consideration

IN THE CAN: A song that has been recorded but not yet released as a record (and probably never will be)

SONG PLUGGER: Person hired by a publisher to play songs for artists or producers for recording consideration

SONG CATALOG: The name given to the song list of a songwriter, or a group of songwriters, usually accompanied with titles, lyrics, and a recording (work tape) of each song

STAFF WRITER: Songwriter who is signed exclusively to write for a designated publisher

DEMO: Usually a demonstration tape of a song to pitch to a prospective artist

CUT: Means a song has been recorded for release consideration

SINGLE: A selected recorded song that is promoted for airplay. A "single" is usually chosen from a session as the best or most popular song on the session.

ALBUM CUT: A recorded song that wasn't picked for a "single" (but may be chosen later as a "single"—or not)

BILLBOARD, CASHBOX, R&R: Trade magazines that give information on charted songs and their chart position; referred to as the songwriter/publishers' "bibles"

CHARTED: Means the song (usually the "single") has made the list of TOP "100" songs in a specified category

COPYRIGHT: Song protection so when someone "steals" your song … you can sue them!

PRODUCER: One who oversees a music session. The Producer usually hires musicians, books studio, and directs the music session.

STUDIO MUSICIAN: Musician whose music actually goes on demos and records

PICKERS: A name given to anyone who plays any musical instrument, whether it be stringed or not

GUITAR PULL: An event where musicians gather to play, usually, songs they have written to one another

CO-WRITER: When two or more writers collaborate on the music and lyrics to create a song, each individual is usually referred to as a "co-writer."

BREAKOUT SONG: Usually the song a "hit" artist is best known for. More times than not, it is his or her first "hit" song.

MUSIC ROW: A few designated blocks of streets and avenues in Nashville, Tennessee where music is prevalent

AIRPLAY: When a song is played on the radio or television, it is usually referred to as "airplay."

DRAW: A monetary advance against future royalties earned by a publishing company from songs you have written

BMI: Broadcast Music Inc., a licensing organization that collects music royalties and pays them to songwriters and publishers

ASCAP: American Society for Composers, Authors and Publishers— performs same functions as BMI

BULLET: A term used in musical chart position meaning the song is "moving" rapidly up the chart and is guaranteed a higher position the following week

CONTRACT: An agreement between publisher and writer stipulating that the writer's song will be exploited by the publisher for money and with the stipulation that the publisher will manage the copyright

PUBLISHED SONG: A song that has been assigned to a publisher by a writer

MINOR ARTIST: A recording artist who is signed to a "minor" record label

MAJOR ARTIST: A recording artist who is signed to a "major" record label, i.e., RCA, MCA, Warner Brothers Records, etc.

MINOR LABEL: A lower budget record label that cannot compete monetarily with a "Major" label such as RCA, MCA, Warner Brothers Records, etc.

PUBLIC DOMAIN: An older composition whose copyright date has expired and can be used or recorded without compensating the original publisher or writer (Usually the writers of these songs are deceased.)

MAJOR LABEL: Usually run by corporations whose stock is on the **Dow Jones Chart**

BACKGROUND SINGERS: Singers who provide background voices to an artist's recording

SCALE: A set amount of money musicians and background singers are paid for their services

DOUBLE SCALE: The Leader of the Musician Group is usually paid twice the amount for his/her services

ENGINEER: The person in charge of the "sound board" during a music session, who ultimately ends up "mixing" the song

Quotes And Supplements

Quotes from some songwriting buddies of mine and some who aren't (songwriters) that I have shown my manuscript.

You know the expression when you read something, "I laughed, I cried, etc ..." Well, you my friend, hit the mark. We laughed out loud over and over, and Jan was moved to tears over Don Gant's passing.
From your writing, I could feel the fun and depth of your friendship with Don, and the respect and love that you shared. Your loss of a great friend was palatable and translated wonderfully through your words.
Good Stuff, Lathan, Good Stuff!
Much like yourself, it's brilliant, engaging, and has a unassuming and surprisingly humble tone."
—Jim King & Jani

lathan exudes creative energy—you can't help but like the guy, and when his eyes light up, jump right into the writer's workshop.
—austin church

There are some songwriters who can express in a few minutes, something so stirring, so deep, that the song will touch your soul and bring tears to your eyes every time you hear it. Lathan Hudson's song "The Doll Maker" is just such a song. The song tells the story of the most humble but reverent lover, and it will break your heart while healing it miraculously at the same time. His performance of it will stay in your mind forever.
—Christine Reilly

Lathan, this is so brilliant ... it goes beyond telling the story of the songwriter ... the way you describe Kristofferson and Howard and the day, the time in Nashville. Your journey ... GOD how I envy you. How I would have wished to live and see those moments. Wow ... I am crying here. I hope you don't mind if I save this, and read it often. I wish I had known you then ... I wish in some crazy way I had maybe chased that dream I was too afraid to chase, and that my daddy wouldn't let me chase back then. You managed to capture so much in your writing, I envy you, being there, experiencing that. I never did. I get little bits and pieces of the illusion here and there, part time songwriter, full time mom ... you know Nashville ain't what it was ... but it still has that little bit of magic, that little bit of remnant of "what was" ... but every time I go home to California, my heart breaks a little bit—torn between my family and what I am committed to, and torn between what my heart lives for. To create, to be part of a community, full time. Live those moments you had. I don't regret one choice I made, but I do wonder "what might have been."

I am praying this year I get to meet you in person—I am praying this year that all these little things I have missed, and every little dream that people put aside thinking will never come true ... DO. You definitely need to make this book your reality. It's magical. You are so special ... and even though you are clear across the country, every time you have reached out to me, can I tell you how much you kept me going? When I thought I could no longer? I have seen such dark sides of life ... hopelessness ... sorrow. As you get older, you just get more tired ... but I prevail. I believe God has a plan for me.

I am working on something special, and I would love to have you write the foreword for it, if you would. I would be honored. There are not many who truly know the cost it takes to follow your talent, your dreams, and your heart. But you do. And you have watched my journey from afar ... I keep this star under my pillow ... still. Hugs, —CS

Lathan Hudson

Author of Once Upon a Time ... There Was a Tavern Volume 1

Lathan Hudson, born and raised in Sylacauga, Alabama, obtained his BS degree in Education from Troy State University, Troy, Alabama.

In 1976 Lathan and his family moved to Nashville, Tennessee, where he became a staff writer for Tree Music Publisher. During his tenure, he subsequently wrote for Pete Drake Productions and Lobo Music.

During his 18 successful years in Nashville, he wrote over 350 songs, of which 180 were recorded by more than 240 different artists. Four of his songs were Grammy nominees. His songs have been recorded by stars the magnitude of B.J. Thomas, Barbra Streisand, Dolly Parton, Linda Ronstadt, Emmy Lou Harris, George Jones, Elvis Costello, Tammy Wynette, Mel Tillis, Burl Ives, Martha & The Vandellas, Wayne Newton, and many others. Two of Lathan's songs were Number 1 hits on the Billboard charts in the 1980s. *New Looks From An Old Lover* and the #1 inspirational hit *I'm In Tune—Finding How Good Life Can Be*, both recorded by B.J. Thomas, are standards and still garner much radio and television air play. His success won him a place in the Alabama Songwriters Hall of Fame. He still writes songs—his music catalogs in Nashville are still active and every now and then another song gets recorded.

While in Nashville, Lathan collaborated with a creative team to produce *The Jingle Bell Monster*, a package with children's story book, plush toy, and CD of the title song by the Hager Twins.

In 1994 he retired from the songwriting business and moved his family to Florida to focus on his book writing and humor seminars. He is the author of *Thurmond—Permanently Sealed*, a compilation of humorous short stories featuring a character named Thurmond, who, according to Hudson's wife, is his alter-ego. The stories are about Thurmond reminiscing through absurd stories—usually with abrupt conundrum endings.

In 2007 Lathan self-published a children's book, *The Himinamis Bear*, and was co-author and co-editor of a Sylacauga anthology of poems and short stories, *Green Plums, Dye-Ditch Water & The Trash Pile Road*. As always, his co-author and co-editor was Janet M. Moreland. Lathan co-wrote, with Sheryl Paige, the songs on the accompanying CD, entitled *Mill Village Buddies Memories*. Prior to writing his Nashville memoirs, he wrote a non-fiction view of his political thoughts, titled *Fort U.S.A.*

Lathan's talents don't stop here. He has written numerous short stories and poems and is the creator of toys and games.

His hobbies are fishing, golf, softball, and reading (Stephen Vincent Benet, Robert Service, Robert Frost, John Grisham, and books on Zen and Tao Te Ching).

Janet M. Moreland
Editor and Technical Assistant

Janet M. Moreland , an author, poet, and short story writer in her own right, was born in Ohio and now resides in Kentucky. She is a graduate of Miami University of Ohio.

She has been friends with Lathan Hudson for twelve years, and was literary agent for many of his published books. For *Once Upon a Time ... There Was a Tavern, Volume 1* (as with many of Lathan's books), she acted as editor, formatting expert, and technical assistant.

Janet enjoys co-writing, and has published historical fiction with Shirley G. Webb, "The Howell Women Saga"—*Cherokee Love*, *Dance in the Rain*, and *Song of Love*—covering four generations of strong, independent women from 1865 to 1953.

She also co-wrote a book of dark poetry with Lawrence T. (*Confusion of The One*) about a man with bipolar disorder and the painful twists and turns of his life.

Janet's own books are *Spilled Words*, poetry and short stories; and *Taka's New Friend* about California's Ohlone Indians, written for fourth and fifth graders.

Her one son and three stepchildren are the source of much joy in her life. She also has great pride in her five siblings and their spouses and forever thanks them for the love and support they give her.

Earl Culver
Cover Designer and Illustrator

Earl Culver designed and illustrated the covers of *Once Upon a Time ... There Was a Tavern, Volume 1*. As Lathan's lifelong friend and fellow traveler, they have shared many good times and modest adventures, not the least of which include: accidentally playing *semi-pro football* against the New Orleans Saints farm team (Pass Point Steelers 55 - BB Comer High School Alumni Football Team 0); working as manual laborers for the AT&SF Railroad; living on a train car on the Hualapai Indian Reservation outside of Peach Springs, AZ; drinking beer with the Hualapai Indians; fishing on Cedar Creek, Paint Creek, the Coosa River, Lake Martin, and the Banana River.

Earl says, "Best of all has been sharing Lathan's gatherings of singers, songwriters, and musicians for their celebration of country music."

Review
Once Upon a Time ... There Was a Tavern, Volume 1

Lathan ... I cannot tell you have much I have enjoyed reading about your life and times smack dab in the middle of the golden era of Nashville. You hung with 'em all, the stars and the movers'& shakers behind the scene, and lived to tell about it, son!

I don't know of anyone in Music City who made more friends in the business than you did. I am not sure whether it was because of your personality, your songwriting ability, or your athleticism, but whatever it was, you have now blessed us with an amazing book, recalling the hilarious, as well as bittersweet, details of your experience. I only have one complaint ... it doesn't rhyme. ;-)

Seriously, I could not put it down. Congratulations, buddy! I'll look forward to seeing you at the top of the NYT best-seller list.

—Johnny Chance Jones,
Songwriter, Owner of Adventureland Theme Park, Dothan, AL